AN EXPERIENCE
DEFINITELY WORTH
ALLEGEDLY HAVING

AN EXPERIENCE DEFINITELY WORTH ALLEGEDLY HAVING

Travel Stories from *The Hairpin*

Edited by Edith Zimmerman

Published by Amazon Publishing, Seattle

www.apub.com

Amazon, the Amazon logo, and Amazon Publishing are
trademarks of Amazon.com, Inc., or its affiliates.

ISBN-13: 9781477849255
ISBN-10: 1477849254

Cover Illustrated by Thyra Heder
Cover Designed by Adil Dara Kim

Library of Congress Control Number: 2013912321

Printed in the United States of America

Welcome to *The Hairpin's An Experience Definitely Worth Allegedly Having*, an Amazon series for the Kindle (that is now also a paperback book). I asked seven of my favorite writers for essays about travel—on whatever topic they wanted and in whatever format they chose—and am delighted with how the collection turned out. The essays are funny, they're weird, they're moving—there are stories about beaches, aerobics, and canes. About loneliness, connection, sunburn. An unplanned but welcome theme in addition to travel is "relationships"—making them, losing them, behaving in their absence. Although maybe that's just the general theme of everything. In any case, I hope you enjoy, and thank you for reading! Which I hope you do, at the very least because in one essay someone says, in a romantic context, "I heard you had diarrhea and bedbugs," and the more I think about it, the more I think it might be one of the tenderest things I've ever heard.

—Edith

LET US GO THEN

Carrie Frye

I. Aerobics

Here is something weird I did when I lived in Buenos Aires: I did a lot of aerobics. My favorite class was at 6:30 p.m., and when I say it was my favorite, I mean that I would plan afternoon and evening dates with friends around it so that—no matter what—at six o'clock or so every night, I'd be in shorts and tennis shoes cutting across the traffic on Avenida Gaona, with the buses honking along and the late-afternoon light slanting, and the air turning gold and peachy. Gyms are gyms. The same soupy cooped-up smell when you walk in one everywhere. Flash a membership card at the front desk, bypass the weight machines downstairs with the bulky guys in their weight-lifting belts, and then climb a flight of stairs to the aerobics room. I'd sit in a corner of the room in a group with the other girls in my class and speak my deplorable Spanish to them and understand about half of what they chatted back to me while the 5:30 p.m. class finished, and then we would all get up and do step aerobics together. Step aerobics—that's the kind where you leap up and down off little platforms—was huge at the time, and this class was the nutso apex, with these long, complex routines, and every so often the teacher would bark into her mic something like, "Now cut the routine in half and do it from the halfway point backward, and then return to the halfway point and go forward again, and then do it once more, but this time straight through from start to finish." If you're a fellow former aerobics-goer, this is not an exaggeration. I have never been in another class like it: it was like doing a Sudoku that would sometimes make you vomit. But we all seemed to take this swooping martial Lost Boy joy in how hard it was, as if being good would eventually lead to recruitment overseas as part of some elite fighting corps of step-aerobics masters ("Yeah, that's right, I just grapevined all over your ass, motherfucker").

Why did I love it so? There was this amazing, resounding clomp when we would all jump onto our steps at the same time. The windows would be open. It was salty pampas southern-hemisphere summer. At that time of day, traffic was ticking up outside. The sidewalks were filled with all these guys (young boys, teenagers, middle-aged men) in groups of twos and threes and fours on their way to play soccer. How many hidden soccer fields around the city hold all the amateur male soccer players of Buenos Aires? Some astounding number. On the corner was an Esso, with red-and-blue branding just like an American Exxon, but also a place with tables where you might go hang out and eat ice cream. (I spent Christmas Day reading there because it was open and air-conditioned.) Everyone else would have their doors and windows open, too, all along the street. The lady who ran the block's little market would be standing outside, and her son would be racing back and forth up and down the sidewalk. You could see the bakery, and the one produce stand that was okay but you were probably better off walking up a couple blocks and over one street to the next one. However, the very best thing on the block was Soul Pizza, which was a completely ordinary Italian restaurant like hundreds of others across Buenos Aires except for its name, which, again, was Soul Pizza. I'm not sure why, as no one associated with it spoken English, and my contribution to the great ongoing exchange of pageantry and cultural understanding between the earth's nations was to teach people I knew (Argentines, Koreans, Germans, Brazilians, etc.) to call it *Souuuuullll Pizza*, like the announcer at the beginning of *Soul Train*. This restaurant was manned by two laconic silver-haired Italian dudes in their sixties with identical beaky noses (brothers, I assumed), who seemed to like me mostly because I never asked them to change the TV channel from what they were watching, and to whom I had once sung out, in a moment of misplaced confidence in my Spanish, "You were terrific tonight!" when I meant, "The meal was terrific tonight!" so it came out sounding like a sexual innuendo, and we were all three sort of startled. And in this neighborhood—not rich not poor not fashionable but slightly frumpy and comfortable—I belonged for that one upside-down summer in some goofy, provisional way, such that when I walked around I felt, after the first couple of months, what a foreigner hopes to feel, which is completely and wonderfully unremarkable. Just another part of the landscape.

II. Metamorphosis

This was 1996. I was twenty-five years old. No email, no Facebook; it cost a dollar a minute to talk to me, so every phone call from the United States was a big event. I told everyone I was in Buenos Aires to write a novel, and that was halfway true. But the entire truth was, I'd had a wretched breakup in Asheville, North Carolina, where I'd been living. Shortly after the breakup, an old college friend, Herschel, had phoned and said he'd won a Fulbright to live in Buenos Aires for a year to study Borges. He was over-the-moon excited. At the end of the call he added, almost as an afterthought, "Hey, maybe you should come, too," and I immediately said, "Yes." Not "Oh maybe! That sounds fun," but just "Yes,

I'll go." It had to have been bewildering, like putting an exploratory line in the water and instead of feeling a tentative tug back, a fish leaps out of the water and onto your boat and says, "Oh my god, I *had* to get out of there, where are we headed?"

I was gone, all in all, about seven months—two months at a language school in Quetzaltenango (or Xela, pronounced *Shay-la*), Guatemala, and five months in Argentina, with a couple of side trips during that time to Uruguay and Chile. As a travel arc, yoking Guatemala with Argentina didn't make much sense—I had to fly back to Miami to get from one country to the other—but I wanted to see Guatemala. It seemed like a place to which people I knew were constantly rappelling back and forth, and this way I could learn a little Spanish. (I spoke only high school French, which was great for making obscure Isabelle Adjani jokes but was otherwise fairly useless here.) The detour to Guatemala also meant I'd do a leg of the trip on my own, so I wouldn't be wilting all over my friend when I got to Argentina. After I bought my plane tickets and paid the school tuition, I had about $4,000 left, an amount I'd somehow squirreled away from a couple of dreary writing and editing jobs, and that, along with a little money from tutoring English in Buenos Aires, is what I lived off. I looked scraggly by the end, but I managed it. I'd spent the year before reading through the Carlos Fuentes shelf at the Asheville library, and I was halfway through the Mario Vargas Llosa shelf. My knowledge of Latin American literature was broad and, to anyone well versed, surely shallow, but my interest and admiration were entirely sincere. I was reading a lot of Gabriel García Márquez (and Rushdie, and Angela Carter, who felt like English-language cousins, once and twice removed), and I wanted to do what they were doing—something big and bursting—and in that context, learning Spanish and sitting in a room in Argentina to write a novel about Wisconsin made sense, at least to me.

Still, it was all a little drastic and randomly chosen.

There's that thing in Greek myths where a person, often a woman, becomes something else. She was a woman and then she's a white cow. Or one day she's a woman and then she's a fish, a tree, a spider, a stream. That's the closest I can come to describing the breakup I'd had. Unlike most things, it never became a funny story. There was a before and an after. Things had gone well and then they hadn't. He loved me and then he didn't. When I think of that time, it's as this person who didn't know who or what she was now. I felt a thousand years old. I felt creaky. I didn't expect the trip to change that, and it didn't, but it seemed like a chance to see what this new thing I had become was. While I was away, I thought about my old boyfriend continually. It became a habit to think of him almost as if he could see me, to wonder if he was imagining where I was and what I was doing, and to see myself in that moment the way he might see me—and to judge myself accordingly. So even though we weren't in touch and he probably wasn't wondering, it became very important to me that entire trip to appear to be doing just great. How are you doing, young woman, in your new life as a fish/a spider/a tree? A-OK. Just fine. Completely good. I haven't had a real conversation in days, but I know where the bus stops are and I know how to get places. I can march around the neighborhood every morning with the landlady's dog and people wave hello to me. I've gotten really good at aerobics, did I tell you?

III. The Rules of Travel

This makes it sound like it was sad. It wasn't sad, the trip. Or it was sad, but I was deeply happy during it. Or it was sad, and I was deeply happy later that I did it. Something like that.

I should probably insert here, I grew up in a family that loved to travel. This was true of both my parents, but my dad especially. He was, for most of his career, a traveling sales rep for a paper company in Wisconsin; that occupation became, even later in his life, after he'd moved into management, an explanation for how he was. He was a charming, pragmatic guy; he liked talking with new people, making small talk and jokes, sizing up what was what in each new place. My mom started taking me along on trips with him when I was two weeks old. I spent a lot of my childhood sitting on a suitcase with a book, listening to him chat up strangers. Once, when I was in third grade, we were on our way to catch a train somewhere in France, and I was lurching along behind him because I'd over-packed and my suitcase was heavy (third grade! I don't know what I had in there, an evening dress?), and he got impatient and said, "Now you know: *never* pack more than you can carry." This still feels like solid advice, and almost like a quasi-existential rule for getting through life. He had lots of others, the Dana Frye Rules of Travel. In addition to travel light, there was arrive early, plan for incompetence, don't complain, be polite, be friendly, and keep an eye out. Good manners were so important around our house that when I got thrown the ball in kickball at school, I'd yell back, "Thank you!" So: only so-so on "adaptation of manners to local customs," but the rest of it I had down pretty well.

The part of the trip that was hardest and most frightening—in Guatemala, when I was traveling alone and spoke the least amount of Spanish—feels, in retrospect, like the most gratifying part, and this stemmed, aside from affection for Guatemala itself, from all that childhood training being activated and put to work. Whatever else had changed, this was still something I was good at. I remember having this twinkling feeling of *Ta-da!* whenever I'd successfully navigate from some new point A to point B. On the plane ride from

Miami to Guatemala City—when I was listening to conversations around me and it was sinking in that two weeks of listening to "Learn Spanish!" cassettes in the car had not magically transformed me into someone who understood what people were saying—I kept opening and reopening the guidebook to study the maps of Guatemala City and Xela, figuring out how to get from the airport to the hotel I'd picked out, how to get from there to the bus terminal the next morning, from the Xela bus terminal to a hotel, and so on. Each little grasshopper skip: *Ta-da! Ta-da! Ta-da!* And near the end of my stay in Xela, when I came down with a miserable cold and had a roll of three-ply Cottonelle toilet paper stowed away in my luggage and could pull it out and honk my nose into all its soft absorbent luxeness? *Ta-fucking-da!* When I brought it out from the back of the suitcase, it felt like I had never seen anything quite that white and puffy before.

IV. La Casa del Último Adiós

When I was in Guatemala, it was at the extreme tail end of their civil war. The school I went to was a leftie activist place; it was understood that the phone in the office was tapped. The teachers were wry, smart, challenging, and a little understandably bored with teaching waves of American college kids how to conjugate basic verbs. At one of the first talks I went to, I remember being thrilled to pick out the word *socioeconómico*. There's a journal entry a couple of days after that ostentatiously marked *domingo*. (Watch out, Gabo, I am on your heels!)

I stayed with a family that had four little boys under the age of eight, my favorite of whom, Otto, the second eldest, once, while eating a piece of his birthday cake, rolled his eyes up into his head and said *"Que rico"* in a way that remains movingly expressive to me of pure and total radiant enjoyment. Despite Otto's example, I continued to "speak" "Spanish" "like" "it" "was" "a" "made-up" "thing" "which" "was" "awkward" "and" "I" "don't" "know" "why" "I" "was" "so" "shy" "and" "weird." My status in the house was something like a taller fifth son who wasn't the brightest and who snuck into the bathroom really early every morning to take a shower. I knew it was wasteful and the water was freezing, so it was not a pleasure, but I'd started giving off a strange odor, which might have been because of the change in diet or from being anxious in a new place or maybe was some sort of hellish second puberty visited on dim fifth sons of the house.

Every day I left the house and saw volcanoes—a row of them, blue, at the edge of the city—on the walk to school, which I never ceased to find thunderstriking, and I'd cross the main city square, eating a piece of bread and feeling pretty happy with life. Xela is the only place where I've ever thought weak instant coffee with lots of sugar stirred into it tasted good. There were tons of stray dogs roaming around the city, and I was fascinated by one guy, clearly homeless and permanently solitary, who walked around everywhere with a pack of them around him in loose formation. I worked on my vocabulary flash cards and translating *The Story of a Shipwrecked Sailor*. I started to know and recognize all the expats in town. I went to discos and did the Macarena at 3:00 a.m. with unironic pleasure. I got stupendously drunk a lot. I had almost-relationships that included sentences like "I heard you had diarrhea and bedbugs," which, while accurate, wasn't something I was used to hearing directed my way romantically, and "I'm confused about monogamy," which sounded more familiar. I took buses to different places and tried to describe everything I was seeing: "The men in the town wear bright red pants, a striped shirt with a hot-pink embroidered collar, and a sort of Panama hat with an embroidered band," etc. Also, I was very sick once in Huehuetenango, and down the block there was a funeral home called La Casa del Último Adiós and that seemed supremely funny. I don't know why. *Que rico.*

My last week in Xela coincided with that of two friends I'd made, Leila and Gabe, both from North Carolina too, and we got this idea to take part in a hike being planned from Xela to Lake Atitlán. This was a distance of about fifty miles and that didn't sound too far to walk; we'd been to Lake Atitlán by bus and it was a short trip. Leila had a crush on one of the guys who was leading the trip, and, after a couple of months of eating starchy food and drinking beer, neither of us really fit in our pants anymore (we called this Papas Ass, for potatoes, and pretended it was like a line of jeans you could buy: "Oh these? Papas Ass jeans"), and two birds one stone, right? There is no way to emphasize enough how hugely unfit we were for this journey, with our too-tight Papas Ass jeans and our vague hopes of getting laid. One thing: it was the rainy season, and I didn't have a raincoat. The way wasn't along any established route, but was mostly an as-the-crow-flies pass up and down mountains and through forests from point A to point B. The morning I was leaving, with my gigantic backpack on, the husband of my host family could barely stand up he was laughing so hard. There were maybe ten of us on the trip. Leila, Gabe, and I shared a tent, and at the end of the first day we were so tired and blistered and it was raining so hard that, after we ate dinner, we stuck our plates and forks outside the tent door to wash in the morning. In the night we heard wild dogs moving through the camp and then finding the plates and licking them clean, and in the morning we were still so tired, we sat on a log and *ate off them anyway.* And then we stuck the plates and forks in our giganto backpacks and hiked some more. *Ta-da!*

That hike was fantastic and miserable and maybe not quite safe, and I dreamed about it for months afterward. At one point Leila and I were way behind the group, and she was scrambling up this hillside in front of me, just clawing her way up, handful by handful through the dirt, and up over her head I could see a black bull with a big gold ring through its nose, like a cartoon bull, looking down from his mountain shelf at us. Guatemala is small, but in its diversity it's like some gorgeous continent that has been radically shrunk and then scrunched up, like a Kleenex, to make mountains. Our route passed through a series of microclimates. There was this miniature cloud forest you'd be climbing your way up along, and then you'd be out on a saw grass altiplano, with little purple flowers everywhere, that felt so lonely and beautiful, it was like wandering through some misty afterworld, and it kept changing like that, one landscape becoming another becoming something completely else again.

V. The House on Gaona

My landlady in Buenos Aires was Marcela. My friend Herschel arranged a room in her house for me, which I could rent month to month, as I still wasn't sure how long I was staying. It was in the neighborhood of Caballito, in the center of the city. My room, which was on the second story, was salmon colored, with high ceilings and a desk to work at and a big old wooden bed with a cream coverlet. There was an immense wooden wardrobe in which my tiny collection of clothes, laid out and hung up, looked swallowed, and a gas heater I was afraid of and rarely used, and so it was a relief when the weather got warmer. The room shared a small connecting kitchen and bath with another room, occupied during the time I lived there by a Berliner named Dirk, a philosophy and literary-science student, and then an American, Jeff, a DJ who was seeing a woman who gave tango demonstrations in San Telmo. Downstairs there was a Viennese architecture student, Andreas, and of course Marcela. I was infatuated with Andreas, who was tall and kindly and looked beautiful in dress shirts, like some handsome Austrian jungle gym.

My room's exterior doors opened onto a tiled patio, a smaller version of the courtyard below, with lots of flowering things growing everywhere, which was a nice, restful place to smoke and drink coffee on. I usually kept my doors open, unless I was writing, so the sun would come into the room. In the afternoons you could hear the "rah-rah-rah" of mysterious hidden soccer fields. If you were drinking wine out there in the evening, you could look across the street and see, in the line of other city buildings, an upstairs gym where women were leaping and waving their arms around, doing aerobics. (I was told this could be funny.) Rent was $400 a month, under the table. (In 1996, the Argentine peso was fixed to the dollar. One peso, one dollar.) It was one of the prettiest places I've ever lived in. Marcela's main source of income was from her work as a set designer for theater and films, and her house had dimensions like an arty theater set. She used toilets and bidets as planters. There were three cats to pose picturesquely about. It was all arranged just so, except for Liza, the dog, who was mournful and barky . . . and unbeloved by the household. "Shut up, Liza" was like the "Good night, John-Boy" of Avenida Gaona.

Marcela herself was theatric: extremely vivid and entertaining and autocratic. She was one of those people who disguised a certain amount of inner flintiness with extravagant expressions of warmth and attachment. Though everyone else in the city said *"Chau chau"* or *"Chau chau beso"* for good-bye (the Spanish version of *ciao ciao*; Buenos Aires had a strong Italian strain), Marcela would say, *"Chau*

chau chau chau chau chau" and *"besos besos"* and throw kisses at you when she was clicking off in her heels to a party and would be back in a few hours. Theater people!

Marcela had a mysterious arrangement with her husband, Javier, a puppeteer in Spain, wherein they saw each other only twice a year: once in Spain, once in Argentina. It was difficult to judge whether this was a sign of sophistication or estrangement. We housemates would speculate about it. It had seemed obviously like a formal empty arrangement, but, on the night before the yearly visit to Spain, we all stayed up until 5:00 a.m., drinking, talking, and smoking on the patio, and Marcela was nervously fluttering in and out of her rooms, packing and dragging suitcases to the street door and sitting down to drink with us and then springing back up, and at one point had me come into her living room to look at the presents she had for Javier (I remember two nice embroidered shirts)—all uncharacteristic for her. The next morning Andreas and I saw her to her cab, and she was shouting directions and throwing *besos* and yelling *"chau chau chau chau"* out the window as the driver, openly rolling his eyes, pulled away from the curb.

VI. The Narrative of Arthur Gordon Pym

One of my favorite books as a kid was called *In a Blue Velvet Dress*. It's about a girl who has to stay in a strange house far from home, and she runs out of books—at one point she starts reading the phone book—and then a ghost in the house where she's staying, the girl in a blue velvet dress, starts leaving books for her, and it's marvelous. I don't know why it was so satisfying to read about books within books, but it was.

Every place you travel should offer this ghost-books service. Before I left, I spent a lot of time worrying about what I'd have to read in Argentina; I'd spent a summer in Paris in high school and run out of books and, in desperation, plunked down twenty dollars (about a fifth of my spending money) for a paperback of *Cujo*. For this trip, I had a Spanish-English dictionary and a verb book, a couple of guidebooks, and *Roget's Thesaurus*—so already, five books but nothing interesting to read. What I hadn't factored in was the free-floating book exchange among travelers, and how random books will wash up into your life from it. *Bleak House, Gravity's Rainbow, Ulysses*: everyone seemed to pack the densest bricks they could. I had *The Complete Works of William Shakespeare*, which no one asked to borrow. The hardest night of the entire trip was the second one, in Xela; I felt severed from my life at home and scared and cold, like an entire Brontë novel wrapped in a windbreaker, bawling in a damp hotel room, and my journal only mentions: *I then read* Two Gentlemen of Verona. I don't know what to tell you—except, I guess, what's ridiculous about us is also what protects us.

But in Buenos Aires, there was a small library run by the American Embassy. It no longer exists, as far as I know; it was shut down my last month in the city because of budget cutbacks in the States. This was during Clinton's first term. The terrible Welfare Reform Act had just passed, and I suppose it didn't seem like a great use of tax dollars to keep a library open so that Americans in Argentina could access old paperbacks of *Foundation*. The library was called Lincoln Center, and it was one long L-shaped room, fluorescent lit. The collection was haphazard but enough: James Thurber's *My Life and Hard Times*, James Baldwin, Edith Wharton, along with the snoozy *Amazing Ships of the US Navy*–type books that always accrete in libraries. It didn't have a bathroom, so it felt like the McDonald's next door was corporate underwriting that part of things.

This was where I went one week to find Edgar Allan Poe's *The Narrative of Arthur Gordon Pym of Nantucket*. It had come up in several conversations around then, always with Argentines. Someone had mentioned it at one party, then someone else had at another. The women in my aerobics class were openly incredulous that I had never read it. I'm not even sure I'd heard of it before, but now it took on an ur-book significance. So I read it, and it seemed clarifying, revealing—in that way that if you like someone and you read their favorite book (or listen to their favorite music, or watch their favorite movie, etc.), you can feel afterward like you figured out something about them. Not everything, but one dimension. And so to the extent that I made sense of Argentina for myself in those five months, it was because of knowing how crazy people were about Edgar Allan Poe and *The Narrative of Arthur Gordon Pym*.

If you haven't read the book, it's the story of a young man named, yes, Arthur Gordon Pym, who stows away in the hold of a whaling ship belonging to his best friend's father. First, a mutiny takes out much of the crew. Then a vicious storm comes, and that takes out everyone else (including Arthur's poor dog) except for four survivors. They float along, starving. They draw straws, and the one with the short straw is killed and they eat him. (Arthur faints during the actual stabbing, so he's not overtly implicated.) Then Arthur's best friend dies from an injury he sustained during the mutiny; his arm is so rotted with gangrene that by the time he dies, it falls off as his body is thrown into the sea. The two remaining men float farther and farther south on the wrecked remains of the boat, until they're picked up by a passing ship. Then everyone on this new boat is killed too—Arthur has awful travel luck—when the crew gets massacred by the natives of a very strange Poe-ish island at the edge of Antarctica. At the end, Arthur's floating in a canoe on a milky, flickering South Pole sea as ash falls from the sky and a curtain of mist opens before him.

Put another way: it's a story about finding yourself at the southern tip of the world by unhappy fate, bereft of friends and everything familiar. The novel is Gothic and sad and gruesome, and, I imagine, the only thing that Poe could have done to make it even more appealing to an Argentine audience would have been to have Arthur stop on an island where Italian dowagers in fur coats walk their tiny white poodles up and down the dog-shit-speckled streets in front of their apartments all day. Oh, and maybe one scene with gauchos.

Although, if Buenos Aires seemed fraught and melancholy, I could never tell whether it was because I was depressed, the people I knew were depressed, or the city itself was depressed. There was a recession under way then, a less severe one than the recessions that followed but still an observable fact of life. The fruit you could buy got stonier; and the restaurants had all these empty tables out front, even late on pretty nights. Near the end of my stay, I went to an ornate gilded café with Andreas to celebrate something or other. It was a spectacular place, with a high-vaulted painted ceiling and waiters stationed in the archways in immaculate-looking starched white jackets. But we were the only people there. When our waiter, who was very old, brought the coffee on his silver tray and was setting out the cups and sugar, you could see where his white jacket had worn out at the cuffs.

Another time I was on a bus with a friend, and this crowd of young *porteño* women walked by, swaying along on their high heels and in the black tight-like leggings all the women were wearing then, and my friend leaned his head against the window and said in a tone of utter desolation, "It used to be so exciting, and now I feel like I never want to see another labia."

VII. Do I Dare?

Seven months is not long to be gone, really. I did aerobics. I learned how to cook a pretty good omelet. I chose a city soccer team to root for (Boca, because Maradona). I worked on my book in a driven, unhappy, sometimes exultant way. I walked poor demented Liza around the neighborhood as a break in the mornings. In the afternoons I'd take these longer, slightly obsessive walks around the city. I would pick out a map in the guidebook of a different quadrant of the city, and then just walk my way in and out of the map, up and down and around all the streets. Sometimes a friend would meet me at an end point and we'd eat a late lunch or sit in the park together. I got used to thinking about people by their names and nationalities—Henri the Swede, Vasha the New Zealander, Eliza the Australian—like something written on a name tag in thick black marker, and having these intense blossoming friendships that were the entire hothouse life span of a friendship packed into a couple of months. I caught fleas from the cats. I smoked too much. My mom came for a visit, and Marcela threw her an afternoon tea party, and then Andreas brought out some schnapps and we all sat around and got schnockered into the evening, and it was lovely. I started to think about returning home. I'd reached that pivot point where you either dig in and stay somewhere—get a job, get a one-year lease—or pack up and go.

As a last side trip, I went to see Pablo Neruda's three houses in Chile: in Valparaíso, Isla Negra, and Santiago. It was about an eighteen-hour bus ride from Buenos Aires to Valparaíso. My plan was to start there, at the house farthest north, and then work southward to Santiago. From there I'd cross back across the Andes to the city of Mendoza, where my friend Eliza would meet me for a couple of days, and then we'd take the bus back together to Buenos Aires.

Before I left, a letter came from my old boyfriend. A couple of days later he phoned. When I saw the envelope lying with the other mail and recognized the handwriting, it seemed like I'd known it would be there. On the bus, I thought about what to do. And then I'd thought about it some more, as I darted in and out of Pablo Neruda's houses and found the different buses and sat on the beach in front of Isla Negra, reading on the rocks. On the one hand, the thought of seeing him when I got back made me feel drugged and heavy and scared for myself. On the other: I called him from a phone bank in Santiago—and what was I doing? And underneath this churn, there was a way in which, deep down, I knew it didn't really matter, because there I was, darting in and out of Pablo Neruda's houses and finding the different buses and sitting on a beach in front of Isla Negra, reading on the rocks. The sky went on forever. The sea went on—if not forever, a very long way. So one day you're a woman and the next you're a white cow and then something else turns you into a spider and then a fish. You're all of them, it doesn't matter. You're the thing you keep turning into. You can find your way.

ON TRAVEL AS AN ESCAPE FROM UNTENABLE CIRCUMSTANCES

Maria Bustillos

One romanticizes the idea of traveling to a distant country, but in my experience the romance-novel version of travel occurs rarely, if ever, in an ordinary person's life. Even if one manages to plan everything out, with gorgeously tempting color brochures and guidebooks lovingly marked up in advance, the likelihood is that unforeseen circumstances will interfere with even the most carefully laid plans. Far more often, though, travel

is inescapable, the result of disruptive, oppressive, or even scary circumstances of one kind or another. A new job, imperatives of family, of education. Or of love.

This is Edward, circa 1984.

When we met, Edward was gay and I was married. He turned up at my house one night in the company of a friend. By means still not entirely clear to me, Edward and I fell, or really more like plummeted, in love. He was twenty-three, and I was twenty-two.

Eventually I moved from LA to San Francisco to be near Edward, who was flaking off in school at Berkeley at that time and working at the university newspaper there, the *Daily Cal.* There was a lot of nightlife, and a lot of reading. Edward is a wonderful dancer, loves a good cocktail, a good novel. He taught me to swing dance. He is a very brilliant writer, and reader. I took a job in the Europe Middle East and Africa division of the travelers cheque department of a bank. I dreamed of writing a novel myself, one that Edward would love. Did I want to do banking? No, not really. Not in the slightest. I wanted only Edward, Edward.

My tiny corner apartment looked out onto Market Street; it was in a lovely and suitably romantic building reminiscent of a wedding cake—tall and white, a gigantic Deco confection full of enormous transvestites. I would marvel at them in the old-fashioned elevator, the kind you shut with a gate: so tall, the size of their shoes! The only transvestites I'd seen up close until then had been in Brazil: delicate, slender ones indistinguishable from ordinary women. I've never forgotten those Amazons, so resplendent, making their way so joyfully, in that much less forgiving world.

My tiny place had high ceilings, a very good hardwood floor, and a lovely '20s bath with walls tiled in a lurid turquoise, glistening black tiled borders, and a quarry tile floor. The bedroom was decorated with Christmas lights and blown-up photographs of Edward; the very walls were beautified with images of my boyfriend, reflecting the condition of my psyche, I was that obsessed.

It wouldn't be fair to blame Edward for the maelstrom of those days. I should give credit where credit is due.

Little miss pleasure seeker!—I have so many things to explain to her. But what would I say, what could I say. I would wind up just rolling my eyes heavenward. Silently implore.

I'd been through a dark patch when I was married that first time. Largely, I had gotten married just to get my (Catholic) parents off my back. They were having no part of the shacking up with the boyfriend thing. The easiest way out, it seemed. Though not for me, had I had a lick of sense! What I ought to have done was just gotten out of there. Please note: getting married never, ever makes anything easier unless you actually want to be married. (In that case, it makes everything immeasurably easier.) But if you do not actually want to be married, things only become worse and more difficult, not less so.

After a short time I found myself doing more drugs than was strictly sensible. Never so much that I couldn't easily manage whatever wacko job I had—private secretary jobs, mostly, for a series of rich lunatics—but obviously too much: drugs every weekend and sometimes weeknights too. I made a new friend, Angelo, a beautiful gay boy a year or two younger than me, who taught me a lot about music; he was a total omnivore and equally scholarly completist about everything from Japanese techno to George Clinton to Cher. Angelo and I went dancing or to shows almost every night. Looking back it was this never-ending carpet of unhappiness, one escape after another.

We had a huge tank of nitrous oxide that I'd have filled at this gas shop in the middle of nowhere. A scabbed, heavy, fearsome industrial-looking thing that I couldn't lift on my own. It made a deafening low-pitched honk when you filled balloons with it at the hard black rubber nipple: very worrying with respect to neighbor-freaking potential. I threw big parties with these huge four-foot monster balloons, people passing out, seeing God, the real miracle being that we were never busted.

I have no idea what possessed me to take such risks. Angelo and I went to the gas place once and there we saw a messed-up-looking dentist in a black Porsche. We were all there to buy gas and after we were finished, in the parking lot, this dentist seated in the driver's seat of his car crazily mimed a balloon at his lips. That shook me quite a lot. Madness, buying drugs at a retail shop—but then, nitrous did seem not so harmful, even if we were all passing out and turning a little blue on the regular. (The song "Love Action" was popular on the radio, and this became the name of the passing out and turning blue, which one would do in a strangely bobbing manner.)

But you'd come to right away, and be fine, sober as a judge in just a few seconds. Unlike cocaine, on which a number of my chums were very obviously making a real mess of their lives at that point. And nitrous was an exotic (if noisy) treat to offer guests— eh, what am I saying, I was out of my mind, there is no other explanation.

I tried to write back then about my nitrous hallucinations.

The nitrous had a sweetish, slightly metallic taste, and was some- how lighter and puffier than air to breathe. The taste was wonderful at first, but a big lungful produced a sensation not unlike nausea, for a moment, before the pleasure rose. And rose, the rainbow-bobbing spiral of the balloon expanding into a chorus of radiantly spangled techno-pop clouds, safe, and happy and sunny. And rose in a spiraling billow of having left the earth and entered the other realm. Fog, colors, beauty all rising and brighter and sharper and then softer and more and more colors. Tendrils of fear rose to brush softly against the ecstasy; getting a little too high, maybe. Suddenly I was like a Macy's Day balloon, fixed-eyed, still, and hugely floating. Sugar sprinkles impressed themselves sharply all inside my skull. They grew and began to rattle like electrified rice. My hair fell off.

"Idiosyncratic is weird wood barn," someone said, far away. And consciousness ended.

[we are the atoms of god, and creation is happening now]

Oh, to be sure. Decades later I would experience some uncomfortable moments, watching *Breaking Bad*, for instance. Considering what I'd briefly become. The weird quasi-logic of drug takers!— when really, the utterly obvious thing to do is knock it off before you really damage yourself like half the waste cases you are regularly seeing around you. Twenty-one, twenty-two, you do not think there is any way such things can happen to you. Somehow I realized they could, or maybe I just became so much happier with the advent of Edward that I didn't want or need drugs anymore.

Anyway. I had become a little eccentric, in my unhappiness, in this and other ways. Spent a long time wearing only gray, black, and white. This austerity was partly to do with knowing I'd made a mistake, and partly a reaction against the generally brash, violent palette of the early '80s. Us would-be aesthetes commonly took an ascetic stance against the gaudiness of the Reagan years, though I don't think I quite understood it as a political position then. Reagan Red that terrible color was called, the aggressive tomato-bomb red of the First Lady and her god-awful Galanos rufflature.

But when I fell in love with Edward, a strange thing happened: I was walking down Melrose Avenue—you can scarcely conceive of the vivid and teeming imagination on that street, in those days—and saw a dress hanging outside a vintage clothes shop, a '50s dress of flowered silk, crimson roses, and lush foliage on a cream silk ground; tight sleeves, a fitted bodice, and a skirt of explosive New Look fullness, swishing and grand. When I tried it on, a glove fit, something shifted deep inside me. Such a cliché, I apologize: Color Had Come Back Into Her Life. But it really had. I would wear that dress until the silk shattered.

In San Francisco, we would dress up and go dancing at the Stud.

Edward would read to me. Could there be anything more wonderful than a tall boy wearing nothing but glasses, reading Evelyn Waugh in a low, musical voice in the middle of the night?

(Sure there could, though not yet.)

But what a boyfriend! This lovely creature in whom I had discovered my other self was a wreck. He had no idea what he wanted to do with his life, was completely at sea; if he had no end of trouble finishing a five-page English paper, how much did the thought of adult life dismay him? It utterly paralyzed him. But for tonight (and there was, always, absolutely, tonight), he would be so enchanting, so witty, a very Adonis, glittering, glowing in every way possible. He was the world to me. Totally unhinged, mercurial, insecure—the kind of boyfriend who would spend the rent money on eye shadow!

For him.

Then my grandfather, whom I giantly loved, had cancer surgery, and I drove home to LA.

He'd been such a powerful guy, Pipo, incredibly tough and strong; even his hair seemed invincible. But when I got down there the day after his surgery, he was all over tubes—in his mouth, tubes in his abdomen, his arms—and he had shrunk down to nothing in the bed, as if he'd been tossed into a pan and reduced by about half. When I'd foolishly had this idea that he would be there all my life, how could he not be? As it turned out, he would recover almost fully, and live to be eighty-seven.

But when I got back to San Francisco, much altered, sobered in a far deeper way than just sobriety from drugs, I found that Edward had burned a big black crater in my bed, having fallen asleep therein with a cigarette. Edward never took drugs, I hasten to add. He was

just gorgeously Magooing his way through things at that point in his life.

The smell was indescribable. My boss at the bank was being transferred to London. Did I want to come?

YES. Even if just to clear my head for a minute.

Edward, broke, still in school, said he would come after me. Yeah,

sure, I thought. Pull the other one, it's got bells on.

So here commenced the only time in my life that I lived alone and single, four months with no boyfriend. London—beautiful, cold, ripe for discovery. I got a library card.

And a tube pass.

I went to the Victoria and Albert Museum and marveled over the netsuke.

I acquired an interest in the collection of William Beckford, to match my interest in his works.

I learned to drink tea, the same tea I still drink every day.

I read.

Firbank, Ivy Compton-Burnett, Hilaire Belloc, more Waugh. Peter Carey's first novel, *Bliss*, gave no clue at all as to what would come from him, in time. Mysteries by the score. I'd hang out in the little South Kensington library for hours, lost, rapt, until they'd kick me out. Last call.

My job was in Mayfair, just a stone's throw from Claridge's. The offices of the publisher Mills & Boon were just down the street. Mayfair is a rich neighborhood, as stately and fine as any in the world. Nowadays one hears complaints of the rich Russians driving up real estate prices; back then it was the Saudis. I'd never seen a woman in a chador or burqa mask before then, but they were a frequent sight in Mayfair and South Kensington in those days.

The office was in such a luxurious neighborhood because it was the place where people whose travelers cheques had been lost or stolen would come to have them replaced. There were five or six girls at individual desks in the big glass-fronted public area adjoining my small office, all of them so pretty, wearing pale blue uniforms very like stewardess uniforms, complete with caps, to help the unfortunates fill out their forms. Sometimes the customers were terribly upset, having just been robbed, or freaked out from having lost not only their travelers cheques but passports, money, everything; it was a delicate job, in a way. But a cushy one compared to the teller jobs in the bank's bigger offices in the City. The uniforms were obviously a drag, made of itchy polyester, and also the girls' hair had to go under their caps. Such a cruel and crazy thing to do to young women, especially in that epoch of big teased hair.

There was a tea lady, Margaret, in her sixties, who wore orangey-red lipstick a little crookedly applied. She was lively and so sweet. She rolled a big tea cart around the office's several floors, probably four times a day. It was awesome tea, really strong and made with the fantastic milk they still had then, which came in glass bottles with foil tops and the gold-topped kind was best, and that was what we always had. The walls of the little cubicle where Margaret answered the phone for everyone were plastered with photographs of all the royals cut from the tabloids. Margaret was plumb loco for Lady Diana. These people, too—it never occurred to me that they wouldn't all endure from everlasting to everlasting.

Since I didn't have to work with the public, I wasn't made to wear a uniform (Margaret didn't have to wear one, either, which complicated matters eventually, as we shall see). My own wild mane was allowed the run of the place. All the girls were far prettier than me, and this would have been evident if they'd been forced into burlap sacks, for at this point it was still perfectly fine to discriminate freely in favor of beautiful women in the workplace. So I was slow to realize that my being permitted to wear mufti was creating resentment that unfortunately came to reflect on my boss, Ron, a really smart and kind Canadian man whom I dearly loved. The guy Stuart who'd been kicked out of the big office when we arrived, jealous of Ron's sudden boss status (Stuart got a still-awesome wood-paneled office upstairs, but you could tell he was "bloody furious"), started putting it about that Ron had imported me from the States, not because he'd taken a shine to me professionally, on account of my being so into computers—the real reason—but because we were Having A Thing. I called my parents in tears. "Well, are you?" said my father, typically. What a joke—I've scarcely ever met a man more devoted to his wife than Ron was to Tess, the incredibly pretty (and just as incredibly rich and nutty) Chinese girl he'd married a few years before.

Telexes flew between London and San Francisco, via a great clanking machine like something out of an Eric Ambler novel, discussing, improbably, the inappropriate nature of my hair in a professional setting. But the mess was all smoothed over in the end by John, the big boss in San Francisco, whose personal secretary I had taught to use the "word processor," and who therefore knew the real reason for the friendship between Ron and me. John eventually wandered over to London and set everything right somehow. After that, Ron had no more problems from that lowlife Stuart. Things settled down really nicely for everyone except him. But I was pretty rattled, and started thinking that maybe the corporate life was not for me.

They were a lot of fun, though, those girls. I couldn't believe how everybody would take off to the pub every day for lunch, in the middle of the day. The Hog in the Pound, the pub was called. Lunch would begin around noon and they'd all stagger back into the office a couple (or three) hours later. I was too much of a lightweight for the daytime pints, but after work—back to the pub! I would go sometimes then. There I tasted my first Pink Gin, a drink I still order from time to time (bitters out), though it's rare to get a decent one here.

During the day, I had gotten the tea habit, but the girls mostly took Nescafé, truly vile powdered stuff made with a lot of milk and sugar in small white plastic cups. Tea was reckoned to be kind of square, an old person's drink. I couldn't get enough of it and still can't, to be honest. Plus, I had tried one sip of Nescafé and gagged, pretty much. We would make one another tea and coffee when Margaret wasn't on one of her trolley runs. "Nice and weak," they would insanely say. And we all smoked like fiends, right at our desks. Friends or business associates coming in from the States would bring me Benson & Hedges Ultra Lights, recently introduced by the carton. Everyone else smoked the purple Silk Cuts, which was like a cheroot in cigarette form. Then as now, American cigarettes were very cheap by London standards, and I liked being able to pass mine out lavishly. The girls didn't care for my sissy ones, though. Once in a while, desperate, one would come by my desk and say, "Can I have one of your fresh-air cigarettes?" with a disarming waggle of her fingers.

My job wasn't very difficult; there wasn't any overtime to speak of. I was mainly a kind of glorified secretary who knew how to use the "word processor" and deal with a bunch of guys from the farthest-flung corners of Europe, the Middle East, and Africa. It was fun. I planned huge lunches and dinners that went on forever, and learned a lot about entertaining. An older Dutch guy I loved, van Reede, whose fingers were deeply stained from unfiltered Camels, liked to shoot the breeze with me at these events. He had nearly starved during the war, told me how they were digging up the bulbs of flowers to eat, in desperation, when the Nazis were tormenting Europe. The sight of a lot of food overwhelmed him, he said, made him uneasy. He told me that he could never pass by a rubbish bin without a pang, even now, thinking he should check out the contents.

Contrary to what I'd heard all my life, I found English food fantastic, even back then. Do they even have sandwich shops anymore? They were the best, but I haven't seen one in London in recent years, so am wondering if they've gone the way of all the little old pubs in the City. I eventually developed the most elegant and perfect lunch ever devised: cheese and tomato on brown, and cucumber and cream cheese on white. That is to say: two crustless thin sandwiches, each barely heftier than a fancy tea sandwich, cut on the diagonal and wrapped in paper. And tea to drink. These beautiful little sandwiches drove Ron insane, though. He was a good trencherman, a little tubby, truth to tell, and after a while he became desperate for a real sandwich, "not these damn hors d'oeuvres, for god's sake." I found him a place on South Molton Street called The Widow Applebaum's that made American-style deli sandwiches that cost a king's ransom. "*Why* don't you just eat like six regular sandwiches?" but he was thrilled to bits with the gigantic pile of pastrami between two loaves of bread, served with proper pickles. (It was very good pastrami.)

I would still have my perfect sandwich lunch every day, if I only could. But ordering it became a slight ordeal because the sandwich guy would give me such grief over my pronunciation of the word *tomato*. Thus it was that I began my campaign to learn to speak with a credible English accent. I practiced like crazy—in my head, out loud, everywhere I went, on the train, with the radio—and changed sandwich shops. I tend to pick up the accent of whomever I'm speaking with anyway; when you're hearing one certain accent all day long, it is much easier to pick up. Weirdly, I had to choose a class to be; I had known but suddenly and deeply realized how language controls class. I chose a slightly casualized approximation of Received Pronunciation, then the regulation BBC accent. Basic Londoner.

It was very exciting to fool my first sandwich guy, who paid me absolutely no notice whatsoever. Triumph! Then I would just "be English" during the day sometimes, buying train tickets or at the shops. My anonymity had become a treasure and I wanted only to observe, never to be a figure of interest or attention. This was one of the most blissful times.

At the pub one night, I confided to Julie (one of the travelers cheque girls, a pink-cheeked vixen from Enfield) that I had learned to pass, and she demanded to hear and test me. Okay, I said, and began speaking to her in my sandwich-accent. Her eyes practically popped out on stalks and she insisted that I demonstrate for everyone, but I demurred. Thereafter at least once every day Julie would appear at my desk. "Talk English," she begged. "Come on, do it, pleeeeease please pleasepleaseplease."

I'd never had the luxury of rising whenever I wanted, of going anywhere I liked, just according to my own inclinations. This alone was intoxicating, and I think back on that time often and with great fondness. Nobody to ask, no one else's needs to consider first. And I say this as one whose happiness consists most in contributing to the happiness of others. Because then you have the other person's happiness to enjoy, plus the knowledge that you are the source of it: a far keener pleasure than the kind you get from just indulging your own appetites. Still—that is a lot of fun, too, and I am grateful to understand very intimately the nature of and difference between these pleasures.

For learning what restaurants and nightclubs to visit, and what books to read, I would buy *Time Out* at the Bond Street tube station, where there was a Lessiter's chocolate cart. I went and saw the Virgin Prunes at the Ace in Brixton (that was a little silly, to go alone to Brixton at night like that) and to the Camden Palace, to see shows alone. Spoke to nobody, drank gin and tonic, experienced elation.

One night I went to see a double feature in Leicester Square, which is right in the middle of town where all the movies are, like Times Square. It was *Taxi Driver* and *Midnight Express*. I was all alone, and it was a black, freezing, rainy night. These are two very upsetting, depressing movies. But so rich and full was my consciousness, the beingness of it, that I remember that night as full of delight as well as darkness, and rain.

Very commonly I would read right through my tube stop (Bond Street). Be late for work, if I didn't watch it.

And then Edward really did come, so suddenly, and took over my iridescent satin trousers. I was so happy to see him; I didn't realize how much I had missed him.

In time we moved to Mile End, to a sort of ghetto full of musicians, news readers, and producers from the BBC. We learned to knit, we knit on the train, learned to play mah-jongg, and went dancing at the Batcave or the Camden Palace on a Thursday night. We learned about astrology, and bought Raphael's *Ephemeris* for our birth years, and astrology forms, and we cast our charts, though far from expertly.

And at Mile End we met a man whom I came to love very much. His name was Brian Ashen.

Brian read the news for the BBC World Service. He was a Professor Higgins to me. He taught me so much about politics, about developing a broad worldview, about the frustrations of the Left, about growing up in the postwar period, about rigor of all kinds—aesthetic, economic, intellectual, and about indulgence as well. From him I learned how to throw a dinner party, the kind that lasts for days. We'd shop forever for a party like this one.

Brian would go to France just to buy cheese on a whim, or *fraises des bois*. His gaiety was infinite, beautiful. I think the word *gay* as the equivalent to *homosexual* was invented for people like him because his effervescence could never have been contained in any conventional form of masculinity. For boyfriends, Brian loved beautiful black boys, far younger than himself. He would rarely invite them over, though, to meet any of us. His life was compartmentalized.

Brian taught me about wine, and how to braise leeks, roast lamb, arrange flowers. And how to decorate a house. His little house was a joy, full

of mementos, slightly ratty chinoiserie furniture, lovely pottery, and many, many books. There was a little garden that he tended with the utmost care, with a fountain in the shape of a lion's head fixed in one old brick wall, water ever pouring from its stony lips.

This is what it looked like from the downstairs window.

In the spring he would plant special plants with the Linnaean names of the boys he'd slept with the year before. Like *Artemisia douglasiana*.

Brian's cats were called Rupert and Jasper.

They would come and visit us all the time, which made Brian mad. There was a big tangle of love at Mile End. Claudine, the clarinet player who left her boring husband, Paul, for Shelly, the lesbian next door—that was a nine days' wonder. Sheila and Duncan, the dog Scruffy. Brian and his boys. Me and Edward.

I idolized Brian (that's me on the right, literally sitting at his feet, my stilettos thrown to one side), but sometimes we'd argue.

One time in particular is deeply fixed in my memory; it was about politics, and I became upset and so did he, we disagreed so absolutely. This is one feature of my character that has never changed: the more I love someone, the more willing I am to contend with that person, until three in the morning, until both of us are drunk and half-crazy. And he said, "This is because *you're* American, and *I'm* English . . . we can never understand one another."

I believe I wept with hurt and anger. "Are you saying that you have more in common with some English axe-murderer than you do with me, who shares, like, *everything* with you?!"

His gaze was so pure and blue. "You're so tender," he said help-lessly. That's the sound of his voice in my mind, saying that. And once when he read George Eliot to us, his favorite writer, describing Mr. Casaubon: "In looking at her his face was often lit up by a smile like pale wintry sunshine." I thought I'd never hear anything so beautiful again, and maybe I never have.

He was already sick by then, though none of us knew it yet.

Brian offered to marry me so that I could stay in England. But what would become of Edward? He wanted to stay in London, but we really had no plan; in those days we were just some kind of aes-thetic flotsam, thinking one day to write, and another day to open a florist shop (Les Fleurs du Mal) dealing in deadish flowers.

In the poem "Enivrez-vous" Baudelaire described our exact condition:

Il faut être toujours ivre.	It is necessary to be always drunk.
Tout est là:	All is there:
c'est l'unique question.	it is the sole question.
Pour ne pas sentir	In order to not feel
l'horrible fardeau du Temps	the horrible burden of Time

qui brise vos épaules	that bruises your shoulders
et vous penche vers la terre,	and pins you to the earth
il faut vous enivrer sans trêve.	it is necessary to intoxicate yourself without cease.
Mais de quoi?	But with what?
De vin, de poésie, ou de vertu, à votre guise.	With wine, with poetry, or virtue, as you will.
Mais enivrez-vous.	But intoxicate yourself.
Et si quelquefois,	And if sometimes,
sur les marches d'un palais, sur l'herbe verte d'un fossé,	on the grounds of a palace, on the green grass of a ditch,
dans la solitude morne de votre chambre, vous vous réveillez, l'ivresse déjà diminuée ou disparue,	in the mute solitude of your own room, you awaken, the drunkenness diminishing or vanished,
demandez au vent,	ask the wind,
à la vague,	the wave,
à l'étoile,	the star,
à l'oiseau,	the bird,

à l'horloge,	the clock,
à tout ce qui fuit,	all that flees,
à tout ce qui gémit,	all that moans,
à tout ce qui roule,	all that rolls,
à tout ce qui chante,	all that sings,
à tout ce qui parle,	all that speaks,
demandez quelle heure il est; *et le vent,*	ask what time it is; and the wind,
la vague,	the wave,
l'étoile,	the star,
l'oiseau,	the bird,
l'horloge,	the clock,
vous répondront:	will answer you:
"Il est l'heure de s'enivrer!	"It is the hour in which to intoxicate yourself!
Pour n'être pas les esclaves *martyrisés du Temps,* *enivrez-vous;*	To not be the martyred slaves of Time, intoxicate yourself,

enivrez-vous sans cesse!	intoxicate yourself without cease!
De vin, de poésie ou de vertu, *à votre guise.*	With wine, with poetry or virtue, as you will.

Not all poems are untranslatable, but this one surely is. The very refrain, *enivrez-vous,* you will rarely see translated the same way twice. "Be always drunken," "get drunk," "be drunk"—no, it's something closer to "endrunken yourself" or "intoxicate yourself"; those are no good either, but this nuance is crucial: this is something one must do oneself, to oneself, with one's own will. The reflexive capacity of Romance verbs permits a compact sense both of volition and of subjectivity in just those two words. You'll will yourself to be drunk, and then you will also be absolutely drunk. So went the poem of my early twenties, my poem of London.

THE LAST GREAT ADVENTURE

Jenna Wortham
Illustrations by Molly Templeton

1.

The guy sitting next to us on the plane to Mexico looked like he'd been dropped in a pot and boiled—his face and chest bloomed in a glorious bouquet of pinks and reds. He was a mess of peeling flesh, so sunburned that when he rubbed his cheeks and chin, long strips of skin came off, and he rolled those pieces between his fingers, making little pill-shaped balls that he dropped absentmindedly on his tray table next to empty minibottles of rum.

We were unfazed. Living in San Francisco had conditioned us to a particularly special breed of weirdo: exotic strangers imbued with a little bit of crazy that was, more often than not, harmless. We were receptive to their nuttiness; most of the time, we liked it. Sometimes we felt like we were tuning into a different human frequency when we talked to these people, picking up a mystical message delivered from an otherworldly oracle, even if we didn't always understand it.

His name was Andrew, I think, and he wanted to buy us drinks. He didn't like drinking alone, he said, and after all, weren't we celebrating? We were on our way to paradise! He ordered four pineapple rum drinks for the row: two for him, one for each of us. We accepted our drinks, raised them in thanks, and drank. He described his business as real estate and said he liked adventure. Did we like adventure, too, he wanted to know. I felt my boyfriend Alex's hand on my thigh—a gentle, persistent pressure— and I had to swallow a giggle. The last time someone asked us that question in that way we were buying groceries in a Harris Teeter in Charlottesville, Virginia. The cashier eyed us while she rang up our food. She gave us a wicked kind of smile and leaned across the scanner, her sagging breasts spilling out of the top of her work shirt. Her hair and makeup were a carnival of crazy colors: bleached blonde cotton candy swirled on top of her head, electric- blue smears above her eyelids, swipes of cracking cinnamon-red across her lips. She asked us if we liked to party and if we liked adventure. Then she asked us if we liked to swing, and before we could answer, she quickly slipped a faded flyer with an address into our bag, between the avocados and the bread. We ran out of the store, laughing, holding hands, elated by the encounter. We never went to the party or back to that Harris Teeter, but we kept the flyer on our fridge and giggled about it for months after.

But this was different; our planemate had a different kind of proposition he wanted to share with us. He said he liked the look of us, the honeymooning type (even though we weren't), and he wanted to help us have the time of our lives. By now we were on our second round of drinks. We told him of our plans to explore the towns around Tulum, and he began jotting down an itinerary for us, describing places where you could swim in caves, the best beach- side spots for an afternoon drink, and the bizarre but authentic (he swore) Italian enclave where you could get Mediterranean-style Mexican food. He told us which bars to go if we wanted to get a little fucked up and the roads to avoid on our way home if we did.

Then he smoothed out a damp cocktail napkin and started drawing a map to a freshwater lagoon, a tiny geographical treasure nestled a few miles past the main bay. Most tourists skipped it, he said, because it was hard to find and there was a much bigger, flashier river park just up the road, where you could see sea turtles, float in giant yellow tubes, and hike around the inlet. But this other place, Yal-ku, was the real deal, he assured us, a great way to laze away a day. You could bring sandwiches, rent snorkels, and explore the tame lake and island, which was dotted with beautiful iron sculptures and attracted schools of colorful fish that wandered in through the narrow inlet that wedded that body of water to the ocean. I studied the napkin and nodded, then placed it carefully between the pages of our earmarked guidebook.

After we deplaned, we shook hands and waved good-bye. We never spoke to him again, but for the rest of the weekend, we would see Andrew lingering on various street corners, talking to people in doorways, ordering drinks in bars, his shirt half-buttoned, face and chest forever lobstery. We always tried to catch his attention, to nod hello or just acknowledge his presence, but his eyes always seemed to land everywhere but on our faces.

We forgot about Yal-ku until our second to last day of the trip. We were trying to decide how to spend our time—whether to drive into town, lie on the beach, or take a day trip. I rifled through our beach tote looking for our guidebook, found it, and flipped through. The folded napkin, now crumpled, fell out. I picked it up and waved it at Alex. We were without a plan, and one had manifested itself in my hand—practically begging us to go, promising to deliver the kind of excitement we craved, the kind of uniting adventure we had headed to Mexico in search of.

2.

We needed something, *anything*, to shake us out of our funk. We'd been living in California for a year or two when we decided we needed a break. The funny thing was that we'd gone to California in search of the same kind of fresh start: neutral territory to claim as our own, since the tiny college town we'd been living in felt like it was closing in around us, with all of our bad habits, exes, and their familiars harder and harder to evade. We drove south first, then west through the dry vastness of the deserts and canyons of Texas, New Mexico, and Arizona before heading north, toward San Francisco. We traced our journey on an oversized foldout map with a pink highlighter and scribbled big black circles over each city we slept in. We used triangles to mark the towns where we saw old friends or made new ones, and put big X's over the swaths of highway where we were followed or stopped by the cops. This was the kind of thing we were good at: conspiring on silly, flash decisions that bordered on irresponsibility, our safety net consisting of little else than each other and a meager shared bank account.

I'd met Alex after my second year of college in Virginia. He was back in school after a hiatus, taking classes to prepare himself to apply to medical school. We were both enrolled in summer school, taking a crash course in physics to fulfill our science requirements. Our class was small, barely twenty people; it was hard not to take stock of everyone that summer. I watched him on a particularly hot day, when a layer of steam seemed to hang over the classroom and everyone sat slumped in their seats, sweating, trying to pay attention to a lecture about entropy. Entropy: the way scientists measure change, the way you quantify spontaneous changes in direction and disorder. Alex was older, handsome, relaxed. Easy. He rarely took notes and was often the first one out the door when class was over. I was barely twenty-one; he was twenty-seven. One day after class, he offered me a ride and that's how it started: his giving me rides every day after class but not always home. "Wanna go somewhere?" he'd ask after we'd already passed the house I was renting for the summer.

"Sure," I'd say, bare feet on the dash, already leaning forward to turn up the radio. We'd drive out to abandoned fields, down dirty country roads, out to newly planted vineyards. We'd listen to music and we'd sit on the hood of his car, talking, and then drive back to town. Those were mini-adventures, just the beginning, and when we started dating a few months later, they grew bigger in scope.

I was in London for a semester abroad when Alex showed up on my doorstep, wanting me to come away to Paris with him for the weekend. I skipped classes and went, and when it was time to catch our train back, I raised an eyebrow when he ordered a second bottle of wine for lunch. He waited, grinning, to see if I'd object or insist we rush back to the station. I lifted my wineglass toward the waiter instead. Afternoon slid into evening. We missed not one but two trains back to London. Alex's flight left for the States without him aboard. Instead, we were in the back of a cab, instructing the driver to make loops around the Eiffel Tower until its lights flickered on; then, we'd decided, we could board a ride home. Another time, during a weekend trip to Vegas, I took too much molly and got lost on a casino floor, mesmerized by the swirling floral patterns behind the blackjack tables. My phone rang and rang; it took five separate calls before I realized where the buzzing was coming from. Alex was on the line; I could only breathily describe the uniforms of the dealers at the table. Within seconds, it felt, he was scooping me up in his arms, laughing and teasing me and kissing the side of my face. We were at our best in those times, partners in crime, fluent in the same language, made up of eye contact and body language. And that was enough then.

We decided to move to California in the same impulsive way. We were drinking whiskey in a bar one night when the idea came up. Let's just move to California, he said, or I said, and it stuck. We couldn't shake it loose. So we picked up extra shifts at the restaurants where we worked, and when I graduated from college, we sold most of our things and packed the rest into our red Volvo and left. But as it turned out, the very best thing about California is also the very worst: it never sheds its skin, never changes, making it even harder for you to cast off your own. I loved it at first, the inertia of San Francisco, marveled at the way we quickly formed a routine and settled into a life, the way we tried to carve out a niche that was ours, and was stunned by how quickly it dulled to look like everything we'd left behind. Even now, some four years after I left, little has changed. The Pacific, eternally hazy and blue; Hippie Hill is always jumping on Sundays. Last time I was back, I walked by the Mix, and Nick, the bartender with the neck tattoo, saw me through the window and lifted a bottle of Jameson like, *Hey, girl, you want some?* And I grinned and shook my head no, and he winked and went back to lining up shots for the crowds of glistening men pushing their way to the bar. The following Monday morning, I glanced up from my laptop in a coffee shop just in time to see my old coworker Sam cruising by on his bike, waving a hand in hello, all casual, like I'd never left and I'd been there all along. Even The Page has that same old gross stain in its carpet, a leftover from when it was called Chances, a dark mess I once fell on, squashing the cheap plastic bird I'd shoved in my hair, mouth blurry from too-red lipstick and too many watered-down drinks I paid for with the previous night's tips from my waitressing shift.

It's deliriously seductive, this sameness, it sucks you in, makes you never want to leave, the sensation of familiar and unfamiliar feelings rising up in you all at the same time. Despite all that's happened, everything that's changed and has yet to change, things somehow manage to be the same. Back then, though, I hated it, the stillness, and itched to leave. Now, I love it. California's topography is emotional, an invisible layer of past moments that hovers over every block, over every bus ride, that you forget about until you're standing right in the middle of a memory, the realness making you weak-kneed with familiarity.

Each time I'm back, I rent a car and spend spare afternoons guiding it down my old streets, retracing the steps of my early twenties, giving myself a tour of my past. *Look, there's the apartment Dwayne and Megan lived in, and that's the bar where we had a fight that kept us out of each other's lives for a year, and the Vietnamese café where we hooked pinkies and promised to be best friends again. And now, coming up on your left, Golden Gate Park. Do you remember that time we wandered into the park at sunrise and a woman was dancing by herself with a boom box to The Cars, and we laughed and let her take a deep pull from our bottle of whiskey and begged her to start the song over and dance some more?* I'm mesmerized by the recollection of moments, perfect little dioramas from that era of my life, but at the time, they felt like tired plays, poorly rehearsed and half-assedly acted, and I grew restless of watching the same scenes play out.

That's how we ended up on a plane to Mexico, which has more to say about us at that point in our relationship than how we ended up in California. We came out West determined to forge a new path, make a new life. We came to Mexico desperate to find our ways back to each other and reclaim part of the original spirit that brought us together. I don't know why we thought we needed to leave to find it. I guess we hoped that a change in scenery, a return to those aimless summer afternoons on sunny country roads, might remind us of where we were and how we ended up there together.

3.

Here's what I remember from our first few days on the Mexican Riviera, which is how all the guidebooks liked to describe the part of the country we were in. The trip got off to a promising start. There were a bunch of Coronas cooling in a bucket next to the driver's seat in the hotel van that picked us up at the airport. Some of the bottles were already drained, bobbing around weightless next to their fuller kin. We were the kind of people who appreciate that kind of thing, so we were the first ones to lift them out by their slender necks, tilting them so streams of water ran back into the bucket and not onto our laps. A few of the other passengers merrily joined us, but I saw most of them glancing at one another nervously, fumbling with their seat belts. We put ours on too but kept rising to get fresh bottles from the bucket. I tried not to get too drunk but it happened anyway, somewhere along the way to the hotel.

I learned a few things about myself in Mexico, like, for example, that I am lactose intolerant. I didn't have the term for it then or know how to stop it, I only knew that every evening, a few hours after happily slurping down creamy piña coladas at dinner, I would be in pure misery, sweating and groaning. It's hard to have a romantic getaway when one person is shitting her brains out every night, but I wasn't clever enough then to understand that my body was rejecting what I insisted on pouring down my throat, rendering me incapacitated for the rest of the night.

That wasn't the only disaster.

On the second or third day of our trip, we decided to go scuba diving. We signed up for lessons, wriggled our bodies into the heavy rubber suits, and got a primer in a lukewarm pool on breathing and the hand signals you make underwater to communicate things like "stay together" and "move apart." We rode out on a big white boat with a dozen or so other students and balanced on the lip of the vessel before falling over the side and into the impossibly blue bowl, exactly like you see in the movies. Felipe, our instructor, deflated our jackets and we sank under the sea's surface. Not long after our finned feet brushed the ocean floor, something went wrong. Alex's weight belt slipped off his slim waist and he was drifting toward the surface, his arms and legs churning, as he tried to get back below. Felipe flashed a palm to me—signaling "pause, stay put"— and headed toward Alex. Within seconds, they had both vanished, and none of the other students were in sight. I waited, both hands clutching a scrawny tuft of seaweed, my only protection against the current that tugged at my body.

Time passed, nothing happened. There was only the thunderous *hunnnghn-hunnngh* sound of bubbles streaming from my respirator to keep me company. Dreamy blue as far as the eye could see. *Hunnnghn-hunnngh.* I tried to keep calm. They would be back. *Hunnnghn-hunnngh.* Later, during dinner, I tried to describe those few minutes when I was alone on the ocean floor, the wall of water curling over my head. It felt like a weird dream I might have about being a specimen in a glass jar—alone and unknown, waiting to be discovered, categorized—that I would wake up from and describe to my sister over text. I waited, hands gripping the torn lace of seaweed. Finally, Felipe appeared, his thin form wriggling down to retrieve me. He squeezed my hand as we returned to the boat, pausing to point out various creatures, a sea turtle, a barracuda, brightly colored tropical fish.

The next day, Alex and I hiked to one of the area's cenotes, large sinkholes of clear, cool water connected to a maze of underwater rivers and caves. We left our shoes and towels on the dirt and waded in. It was colder than the ocean and dimmer, much dimmer. I didn't have my contacts in and I couldn't see without my glasses, so I gripped the pocket on Alex's shorts as we swam deeper in the caves. Some kids splashing nearby told us if we went farther in, around a pitch-black bend and through an underwater tunnel, we would come out into a beautiful, remote patch of jungle. One of the boys, a tender imitation of a man, unfurled himself from the rock where he was lounging to look at us. The sun was already dropping below the horizon, so we had to hurry, he said. He offered to show us. He slid into the water and began swimming, using fast, broad strokes that pulled him away from us and into the darkness. He paused after the bend, and indicated with his hand how we were to swim underwater to navigate the tunnel. He had only one flashlight, he said, so we could make a chain by placing one hand on the ankle on the person in front of us so that we wouldn't get lost. I thought of the stillness of the ocean floor the day before and asked him about the history of the caves to stall. They were sacred, he said, adding that, supposedly, ancient Mayans would throw people in there as offerings to various gods. I wanted to be brave; I wanted this to be a story that we could tell to our friends when we got back, something we could reenact at dinner parties and brag about in dark corner booths of bars. But I froze, in the water, as the two of them swam ahead. Alex turned back and hesitated. I could see the disappointment on his face as he read the desperation in mine, and paddled back toward me. As we swam back to the bank where we'd left our clothes, I skimmed the bottom of the pool for bones, the remains of another kind of sacrifice, but I was disappointed, too, because I didn't see any.

The whole trip wasn't a wreck; we had some lovely moments too. We sang Spanish karaoke and got an unsolicited lesson from a bartender on how to bribe the police if you or your cab driver gets pulled over. We hiked out to ruins and found a deserted patch of sand next to impossibly cerulean-blue water and watched a pack of kids paddling out to surf. The thing about traveling is that you think you'll come back a changed person, a new you, simply by virtue of leaving your comfortable nest and getting into some real shit, enlightened by the ways of the rest of the world. Maybe you want to relax or hope to accrue some intangible wisdom about life and what it all means. You might buy some new clothes or even get a haircut that suits this future you, preparation for the version that will come back reshaped, changed, different. It could happen. It might not. It certainly wasn't our fix for something that was already breaking. By the time we arrived in Mexico, something between us had changed, was maybe already disintegrating. I constantly felt on the cusp of a realization, an awareness I couldn't quite grasp, like the beginnings of a sneeze before it decides whether it'll disappear or come out in full force. Our relationship had knitted together quicker than anyone ever expected and it was unraveling even faster, pieces left behind on the ocean floor and below the crystal waters of the cenote.

By the end of the trip, the mishaps outnumbered the haps, and our desperation to excavate some remnants of the way we were before radiated through our bodies, stronger than the hangovers and sunburns we were nursing. These were the events that led us almost to the end of our trip, when we found Andrew's note and decided that yes, this could be our redemptive outing, a souvenir that doubles as a savior.

4.

We packed a bag with some water, snacks, towels, and sunglasses. We studied the shaky lines sketched on the cocktail napkin and jumped in the car. The road to Yal-ku wasn't marked—we almost missed it. Alex jerked the car onto the rough lot and we parked. We walked toward a woman holding a monkey and smiled. She smiled back and nodded encouragingly. We were on the right path. We rounded a corner and the lagoon filled our vision, a gorgeous green blanket of bushes stretching toward deep pools of water, and you could just see the ocean curving beyond in the distance. Trees dipped down to kiss the gently lapping waves and graceful iron sculptures lifted out of the water. The ocean played against a natural rocky wall, tossing salty handfuls into the freshwater pools, warming the temperature and creating a kind of natural, gently swirling Jacuzzi. Older ladies fanned themselves in the shade, talking, laughing, and swatting at kids when they ran by. A French family with snorkeling gear jumped into one of the deeper pools, four of them in a row, holding hands—mother, father, son, younger son. They pulled their masks down and ducked their faces under, lifting them up again in excitement, pointing and describing what they saw. Their spirits were high and they restored some of ours. The scene was a postcard, a single slide lifted from someone else's perfect vacation. I slipped my hand into Alex's and pulled him closer; it seemed like our world might recover some of its lost density, some of its previous momentum, and I felt dizzy with eagerness to get things back to where they were, to try again to mine the quarry of our former romance. I could feel the bond between us reforming, atoms and particles gathering into an invisible cord tethering us to each other once more.

We pulled our own snorkeling masks over our faces and swam in the warm water, side by side, toward the middle. I could see the soft, silty bottom falling away below us. The air got quieter as the sounds of laughter grew fainter, as the chattering voices faded away. We floated there, drifting in the gentle current. We watched the choreography of life unfolding underwater below, fish darting around, animals crawling along the bottom. Our fingers occasionally found each other's and clasped. I felt the funny brushes on my foot first. I could see big-bodied fish below me, most of them enjoying the day as lazily as we were. You wouldn't think they were the type to make meals out of toes, but after a few seconds, I felt the fluttering again, this time a little more insistent, closer to grasping. I paddled my feet to deter it, and felt them push against something soft and hard at the same time. Something with skin and bones. I turned my head so that my ear was out of the water and skimmed the surface for activity. Nothing but Alex's tanned, lean back bobbing peacefully next to me. Then I heard a male voice, desperate and hoarse. I lifted my face out of the water and I could see a man pointing at something behind me, frantically, and he was yelling. No, he was screaming.

"*Ayúdame!*"

"*Ayúdame!*"

I tore off my goggles and pivoted my body around in the water and came face-to-face with the hard-soft thing I had kicked moments ago. It was a little girl, splashing, struggling to stay above water, crying and choking. Her friends were still sitting on the rock that she must have fallen from, paralyzed, staring down at her thrashing body, their too-short arms unable to pull her back up.

I reached the girl first. I made my body into a seat under hers and used my thighs to push her up and out of the water. What happened next I remember only as a series of impressions. An arm slung around my neck. The mewing, sucking sounds she made as her head came out of the water and the violent desperate sputtering sound I made as my head went down. I couldn't see anything except water trails from her limbs, and my own lungs felt like they were filling with water.

Later I googled and read that when you're trying to help someone who's drowning, you need to restrain their body while lifting them out of the water. That way, in their panic, they don't use your body like a pool noodle and force you underwater. I didn't know that then. What I knew was that I was drowning.

I stretched my legs down and desperately felt around for rocks below to stand on, but we were too far out for anything like that. I bicycled my feet to try to lift us both out of the water, but her arms were around my neck, holding my head below. Hers wasn't clear of the water either. I opened my eyes to see movement toward me, and then I was rising and so was she, Alex's arms under my body so that I could breathe. We both vomited in the water while Alex towed us back to a part of the lagoon shallow enough so that we could stand. The little girl released me and splashed toward her father, sobbing. Activity around the lagoon seemed to resume, but it's possible that it had never stopped, that the landscape had remained indifferent, that no one had ever noticed our frantic episode.

Alex and I helped each other to shore, and sat alongside the edge, panting. The little girl's father rushed toward us, and he took our hands, clasping them between his in a kind of prayer. "Thank you, thank you," he cried, and we gripped his hands back. We picked up our things and walked to our car. We drove back to the hotel in silence, and walked down to the beach. We took in our last eyefuls of the water, the sand, each other in this setting. Things between us didn't feel different, although I thought they should.

Saving one thing seemed like a surefire sign that we could save another, the bond between us and our relationship. That night we didn't go out, we didn't drink too many drinks to commemorate our crazy day and our last night in paradise. We talked about the girl, her family, and what could have happened if we hadn't been there, if Alex hadn't been there. We had a quiet dinner, each lost in our own thoughts. It would be a few more years before our relationship truly ended, but nothing felt the same after that trip. We had our story, a great tale that we could tell to friends over drinks, something that would keep them captivated, on the edges of their seats. But we never told anyone; we kept it to ourselves. I'm not sure why. Maybe because it would be a reminder that we had no choice but to save that little girl, that the decision came from our guts, from instinct. We helped her because we had to. But we couldn't find the resolve to help ourselves and each other, and that was another kind of choice, one that was also beyond our control.

PARIS IS (LONELY/LOVELY)
WHEN YOU'RE ALONE

Chiara Atik

I 've been a dating writer for the past three years. It's not something I set out to do, really, but I liked writing, and had been on dates, and those are apparently the only real qualifications you need.

Being a dating writer consists mostly of encouraging people to date: spurring them on through their pursuit of love, and acknowledging that, yes, the process is frustrating at times but also, ultimately, so worthwhile, because who doesn't want to be in love?

Not that dating is the be-all and end-all. You don't always have to have a significant other, of course. You don't always have to *want* a significant other, either. A lot of times, it's perfectly nice, it's perfectly lovely, to be alone. And I really believe that, despite the thousands upon thousands of words I've dedicated to the subject of dating—the words, and hours, and conversations, and mental energy, and the years of my life I've spent trying to figure it out, both as a "professional" and as an interested citizen. I really do think it's OK to be single. In fact, for the majority of the time I've spent as a dating writer, I have been.

Nine out of ten times, when you tell someone you're a dating writer, they say, "Oh, just like Carrie Bradshaw!" I have an annoying canned response to this ("Only with a much smaller shoe budget!"), which the other person will laugh at, out of politeness. What I don't normally launch into (because who cares, really?) is that the real difference between me and the fictional protagonist of *Sex and the City* is that she spends most of her life either despairing about her relationship or despairing about her lack of one, while I'm pretty at peace with my single status. If you've got a job and you've got an apartment and you've got a friend and you've got dates, then you're pretty much set. You don't need a boyfriend for anything.

Except.

Except. When it comes to travel.

Because as much as I sing the praises of the lifestyle of the independent woman, and as much as I truly do not need some guy to put together my IKEA furniture or zip up a dress or visit my family at Christmas, when it comes to traveling in your twenties and thirties, a boyfriend is practically an economic necessity.

The idea of the lone traveler is romantic, sure, but the economic reality of traveling by yourself when you're my age is daunting. Cost-wise, when traveling as a couple, the only thing that gets multiplied by two is the plane ticket: you'll obviously need two of those. But after that, each vacation expense is halved. Meals on the cheap are more cost-effective when sharing. Car rental is prohibitive on your own but affordable in pairs. A hotel room—the exact same hotel room that a single person would stay in—is half the price when there are two people per bed. The way travel pricing works, it makes sense that the animals on Noah's ark went two by two—it was probably just cheaper to split a stall.

Of course, a good friend, one with whom you travel well, can very easily take the place of a boyfriend when it comes to planning vacations and adventures. But finding a friend in New York who not only has the same travel interests as you but also the same budget and vacation days is like finding a needle in a haystack. And she, of course, would have to be single, too. It's a universal law that people in relationships prefer traveling with each other to traveling with their single friends. (Which is just as well, really: there's nothing worse than spending an hour in the hotel room watching *Murder She Wrote* in some language you don't understand while your friend has a two-hour Skype date with her boyfriend back home. Headset and all.)

While I'm perfectly content to be single in my New York life, for the past few years, as vacation time approaches, so does the pang of not having a boyfriend. Not just a boyfriend, a travel companion. And not just a travel companion but a travel companion with whom I share an incredible romantic and sexual chemistry. It doesn't seem like too much to ask, especially for a dating writer. But the perfect guy—the travel buddy, the adventure partner, the seat 12B to my 12A—has yet to come along.

So when, in the summer of 2011, I found myself the holder of a free round-trip ticket to anywhere in the world, I decided to hold on to it for a bit before cashing it in for a trip to Bali, or Hong Kong, or Nairobi. I bought guidebooks. I did research. I took my time. I think it's because, deep down, I was waiting to use it when I had a boyfriend. It would just be more practical to cash it in when I was seeing someone: that way, we could split costs, and the voyage to Delhi would be romantic rather than just mildly dangerous. I thought I was being forward thinking; I never for one moment considered I'd use my ticket alone.

But by December of last year, the ticket was close to expiring, and I had no boyfriend to speak of, no conveniently rich friend with benefits I could entice into a trip across the world. Resigned, and unwilling to let the ticket go to waste, I started researching in earnest, this time looking for a place I could travel to on my own.

Moscow seemed too lonely to visit alone. San Francisco too pedestrian. I wanted someplace foreign—but not too foreign. Someplace different, but where I'd know the language. Exotic, yet comfortable.

I chose Paris.

I'd been there twice before: once as a grumpy seventh grader with my parents, and then again as a grumpy twenty-year-old with my parents. On both trips, I marched behind them, through the Louvre, up the stairs of the Eiffel Tower, across the Pont Neuf and back to the hotel by 8:00 p.m. to watch BBC News. I wish I could say I mustered up excitement for anything other than the occasional Internet café, but I didn't.

Sure, I had liked Paris well enough, but not that much. And a city I liked well enough but not THAT much was perfect for my current circumstances: I knew I'd like it just fine. But I wouldn't fall in love with it, wouldn't spend the whole time wishing I were sharing it with someone else. I could go there to write—not about dating. About serious stuff.

So I booked Paris—Paris at Christmas, Paris at Christmas alone—and started the extremely satisfying process of casually telling people my holiday plans. It felt sophisticated, renting an apartment in order to write over the holidays with nary a boyfriend or parental figure to speak of. Carrie Bradshaw went to Paris, but she'd needed a man to take her. I didn't.

"Aren't you worried about being lonely?" friends asked.

"No, not at all!" I lied. "I'll probably be so busy," I'd breeze, as though I were heading to France for a business trip rather than an eccentric solo holiday vacation.

I was nervous about being lonely—of course I was. I thought back to a Thanksgiving I'd spent alone, years ago, because I'd had work to do and didn't think it was worth the New York–LA trip for just two days. On the day of Thanksgiving, though, when all my friends were uploading pictures of their extended families and table-scapes, I felt so desperately lonely that I downloaded every single Thanksgiving-themed episode of *Friends* in hopes of finding some comfort in the sitcom familiarity. (And I don't even like *Friends* that much.) In going to Paris at Christmas, I was running the same risk.

"Paris is so romantic!" Others would coo, upon hearing of my plans. This, too, worried me a bit: Everyone knows Paris is lauded as the most romantic city in the world. By going there as a singleton during the loneliest time of year, I was sort of asking for trouble.

But I had spent the better half of three years encouraging people not only to date but to be content with themselves on their own, to not rely on a boyfriend to magically make life palatable, to not let romantic unattachment get in the way of happiness. Going on vacation alone felt a bit like an issue of professional integrity: I had to make sure I could practice what I preached.

With a fair amount of trepidation, and excitement, I arrived at the train station, hailed a cab, and prepared myself for two weeks of solitude.

"You visiting friends?" my cab driver asked me.

"Nope," I said.

"You live here?"

"No, I'm here on vacation."

"With friends?" he asked again, hopefully.

"No, I'm just . . . I'm here by myself."

The driver looked at me from the rearview mirror, eyebrows raised.

"I'm a writer," I supplied, as if that would explain things, at least somewhat.

"You write books?" he asked.

"I just wrote one, yes. About dating."

"Dating?"

"Yes—like, romance, relationships, love . . . ," I said, embarrassed by my own description.

"Ah!" he said, beaming at me through the mirror. "Paris is a very romantic city!"

Yes, Paris is a very romantic city, as I quickly learned during my first few days exploring. There were scores, and scores, and scores of couples (weirdly attractive couples; hotter than the average-couple couples) walking hand in hand, making out with abandon, and generally acting like they were serving as backdrops in a farce of what Americans think Parisians are actually like. But this didn't bother me. I became more and more comfortable with the idea of being somewhere—not just being somewhere but *vacationing* somewhere—on my own. My days were made up of reading and meandering and doing just what I liked. One day I read magazines on the couch till two in the afternoon. Another day I waited in line for the Musée d'Orsay for an hour and a half, then after thirty minutes inside, I decided it was too crowded to enjoy, and left. Every time I saw an Agnès B or Comptoir des Cotonniers store, I went in to look, even though there's one on every corner, and the inventory was always exactly the same. And, in what truly takes the cake for Things No One Would Have Indulged Me in Had I Been Traveling with Anyone Else: one night, I went to the tourist-trappy theater in Saint-Germain that shows old American movies set in Paris. I saw *Gigi*. I loved it.

Aren't you lonely? my friend texted, about halfway through the first week.

No! Not at all, I replied, and this time, I wasn't even lying. "Really, not at all."

Meals were the only things that provided me with any sort of social difficulty. Traveling alone is one thing. Dining alone is another matter entirely.

Breakfast quickly became my favorite meal, mostly because it was the easiest. People tend to either eat breakfast at home or stop in for a coffee on their commute to work. Eating breakfast out isn't dining: it's perfunctory, and can easily be done alone. I started to enjoy the little ritual of going to the restaurant down the street every day and ordering the same thing: a *café crème,* a *tartine* with butter and jam, a croissant, and a glass of orange juice. (A hilariously enormous breakfast, but, like every other American who has ever visited Europe, I convinced myself that I "was doing so much walking" and that it was therefore totally fine to eat eight hundred calories' worth of carbohydrates before 9:00 a.m.) I liked the routine I established (same table, same waitress, same gargantuan order), and I liked sitting there for upward of forty minutes, watching the same people dash in for their morning coffee, writing in my notebook (lest I or anyone else for one second forget that I AM A WRITER), and reading my book. (*A Moveable Feast.* Have you heard of it? It's about writers in Paris.)

After breakfast, I would wait an appropriate amount of time (four hours, if I was able to really distract myself, but more often three) before starting to plan lunch. Lunch is a little more intimidating for the solo American diner in Paris. Parisian women, I could see, had no qualms about eating lunch alone. The sidewalk brasseries were full of them, sometimes surrounded by shopping bags, sometimes reading books, delicately eating their *salades Niçoise* (no, they probably weren't *salades Niçoise*; that's just the only French salad name I can think of, and I certainly didn't order salad the entire time I was there), taking bites of their *croque-monsieurs* (yes, there were *croque-monsieurs*; this I can confirm), and sipping glasses of wine. After their plates were cleared, they would order coffee, take out a cigarette, and sit for upward of thirty minutes. Sometimes they had a book or the paper. Sometimes they would take out their cell phones. But mostly they'd just smoke and stare out at the passing crowds. Yes, French women don't get fat, and that's cool, I guess. More impressively, they're badass when it comes to eating lunch alone.

But even though I could see that enjoying a languid lunch by oneself was an accepted, if not celebrated, part of Parisian culture, I worried about doing so myself. I eat lunch alone all the time in New York, but at, like, Chipotle. Scarfing down a burrito at a fast-food chain while texting the whole time is my normal lunch routine, but something about the *cafés* in Paris, with their tables so . . . visible . . . and the chairs all facing the same way, seemed so exposed. It's like no one even bothers pretending they aren't there to people watch.

There is something uniquely intimidating about a busy *café* in Paris, with table after table of smartly turned-out Parisians (those French men really know how to wear a scarf!), all eyes seemingly trained on you as you bumble through the rows of chairs (*"Excusez-moi! Uhm, pardon!* Whoops! Sorr—*excusez-moi!"*) with your shopping bag from the Musée d'Orsay in one hand and *Navigating Paris by Yourself* in the other. Choosing a lunchtime spot was painstaking work. It couldn't be anything TOO TOURISTY—I wanted actual French clientele. That having been said, if the clientele seemed TOO FRENCH (if you know what I mean), then I would deem it too intimidating/insidery and scurry away, phrase book in hand.

There had to be a table outside, it had to be within reasonable proximity to the heating lamp, the waiter had to look "friendly" (no, seriously), and the menu had to have *steak frites* (which, bizarrely, I could never seem to find).

If I identified a restaurant that might seem like a possibility, I would circle around it like a hawk (buzzard?), sometimes doing an entire loop of the block because I (falsely) thought this was more inconspicuous than just standing planted on the sidewalk in front of it, squintingly scrutinizing it, like I noticed other tourists doing. (Parisians just breezily walk into brasseries without so much as stopping to look at the menu, much like I do in a New York Chipotle.)

After the third (or fourth, let's be honest) trip, once I was *suuuure* that I could expect to dine there and feel reasonably comfortable, I would take my place among the hundreds, and hundreds, and hundreds of solo lunchers.

So I conquered lunch. And coffee in the afternoon, in the evening, and whenever I wanted to pay six euros for the pleasure of sitting down for a moment. I adapted astonishingly quickly to the luxury of just sitting in a cityscape and watching the throngs go by, with no cellular safety blanket to distract me. Yes, coffee, and the meditative repose it afforded me, was quite nice.

So breakfast, lunch, and upward of three or four coffee breaks a day were all taken care of, and I found myself spending my time in Paris well fed, if slightly overcaffeinated.

But dinner. Dinner was another matter entirely. Chic women who served as my dining companions during the luncheon hours would go home to their families at dinner. The bescarved French men that I'd ogle while eating my morning baguette with butter would meet up with girlfriends. And everywhere, restaurants that had once been invitingly set up to accommodate the solo diner, with the rows of chairs facing uniformly toward the sidewalk, were now occupied by convivial *bons vivants*, the chairs turned inward to face one another in cozy, closed-off groupings.

If breakfast is utilitarian and lunch is the respite in the middle of an otherwise busy day, dinner is when Parisians come together. A glass of wine is fine for lunch, but at dinner you order a bottle.

A *croque-monsieur* at midday is fitting, but dinner calls for an appetizer, a steak, and maybe some *crème brûlée*. And after the crumbs have been cleared, a glass of port and a cigarette, one last funny story, and a long walk home, hand in hand.

Dinner in Paris—dinner everywhere, I guess—is meant to be done in twos, or in threes or fours or sevens or eights. Oh, some people can pull off dinner alone—distinguished-looking businessmen, or older women in walking shoes who don't give a hoot what anyone thinks of them. But for a twenty-six-year-old who still cares a great deal about what anyone thinks, it's a different story. Hemingway would have dined alone without a second thought. Carrie Bradshaw might have just ordered room service. As for me, when evening fell, and the restaurants began to fill with families and groups of tourists and boyfriends and sisters and wives and friends, I would slump back to my Airbnb apartment, armed with a baguette and whatever cheese I had meekly pointed to at the *fromagerie*, and call it an early night.

This was Paris, romantic Paris: bread and cheese and book; an apartment that I could pretend was my own; misty streets with the Christmas lights still hanging; miles of store windows to gaze at and apartment windows to peek through; the feeling that I was wholly, comfortingly unoriginal in my pilgrimage here; that feeling you get, while traveling, when no one knows who you are, when you don't belong to anyone, that you can be anyone, untethered to your identity; the fleeting thought of maybe coming back here one day with someone, and what I would tell that someone about my time alone; a smushed *macaron* in crumbly pastel green, a half-read *Paris Match,* an early night. It was romance—I have never done anything more romantic than take myself to Paris.

My sojourn in Paris had given me almost everything—what I still needed was a boyfriend. Ha ha! No, what I still needed, or felt like I needed, was a full meal out. I'm not a foodie, but I had a fantasy of a Parisian dinner, one with steak. And yet, in restaurant after restaurant, I couldn't find *steak frites.* I started to wonder if it was just an annoying Americanization of French food, the equivalent of ordering fettuccine Alfredo in Italy, or General Tso's chicken in Shanghai.

So on my last night in the city, with one final meal in France to go, I turned to Yelp for suggestions. (I later learned, via a belated email from my dad, that brasseries ALL have *steak frites,* even if it's not always listed on the menu.) I googled *steak frites* and *Paris,* and was immediately led to the Yelp page for a place called Le Relais de l'Entrecôte.

I had imagined happening upon some unassuming *bistrot* situated on some medieval street, like the sort of place Anthony Bourdain always seems to find, but Le Relais, from what I could gather, was some sort of Parisian chain. This would normally have been a turnoff, but the reviews reminded me of Californians extolling the virtues of In-N-Out. ("Always my first stop in Paris," wrote one reviewer. "Wish I knew what was in that sauce—best fries I've ever tasted," wrote another.) There's no menu, as the restaurant only serves one thing: *steak frites.* When I read that each customer receives a generous second helping of fries without even asking, I was definitely intrigued. But reading further, the Yelp reviews got discouraging. "Great place for families!" wrote one. "Get there right at 7 when the doors open—it's PACKED!!" This had me imagining some French version of Denny's. Not exactly the place where one goes for a sophisticated meal alone. So I decided to skip Le Relais, for this trip, anyway, and try my luck, once more, on foot.

I left my apartment and began the hunt for the perfect place. There were tons of restaurants, of course, but I was being particular. Someplace nice. Someplace not too expensive. Someplace maybe a little like the restaurant in *Ratatouille*, without the rats. On each corner, I'd see a restaurant, scrutinize it, and decide to walk "just another block," in case something way better was just around the corner. I was afraid to commit to a restaurant—afraid that my one big meal in Paris would be wasted on something mediocre, yes. But also, afraid of looking eccentric. Pathetic. Alone.

Street after street, corner after corner, I kept going until suddenly I found myself outside my usual domain, on a side of the Jardin des Plantes that I wasn't familiar with. I knew vaguely where I was, but not precisely. The stores lining the street all seemed closed, and there were no restaurants in sight. And then, poetically, it began to rain. Looking down at the ground, bracing myself against the drops, I noticed how the lights shone against the wet cement, and thought of a line Éponine sings in *Les Misérables*: "In the rain the pavement shines like silver." The pavement really did shine like silver. And here I was, ridiculously, incredibly, just like Éponine: in Paris, wandering the streets in the rain. Completely on my own.

The entire trip, I'd been happy in my solitude, and not just because I'd willed myself to be so. But suddenly, on my last night, it was raining and I was lost and hungry and wanted someone—anyone! A boyfriend, a friend, my mom—to be there with me, to make a decision, to say, "We're going to *this* restaurant and it's this way."

But I couldn't conjure my mother at that moment, much less a boyfriend. So I kept walking.

And suddenly, the pavement stopped shining like silver, and shone like neon instead. Peering up through the rain, I saw a flashing red sign: LE RELAIS DE L'ENTRECÔTE, which, from the outside, anyway, looked more Moulin Rouge than Denny's. I looked at my watch. 6:49 p.m. Early for dinner, but almost exactly the time the Yelp reviewer had recommended arriving in order to beat the crowds. I had written off Le Relais, but I certainly wasn't going to deny what was clearly a sign (from God? From Hemingway?), so I got in line behind a group of Japanese tourists.

At 7:00 p.m. on the dot, the doors opened and a phalanx of waitresses dressed as—well, dressed as French maids, to be perfectly honest, stood at command. "How many?" One asked the Japanese tourists in front of me, in perfect English, ushering them to a long table in the corner.

"How many?" Another one asked me, in equally perfect English.

"Just *moi*!" I replied jovially. Without cracking a smile, she led me to a small table maybe, oh, six inches from another small table, where a French couple was already seated. I nodded at them as I awkwardly squeezed past them into my seat, and did my best to look nonchalant when a busboy came over to take away the extra place setting across from me.

Another waitress (the same waitress?—the matching Harvey House uniforms made it hard to differentiate) came over to see if I wanted to start my meal with a glass of champagne. Yes. Yes, please. Quickly. The champagne, I figured, would at least give me something to do. There was no menu to look at (it was *steak frites* or nothing, at this place), no scenery to stare at, and even though I was dining alone, I still felt a childlike guilt at the idea of taking my phone out at the dinner table. The French couple and I were settling in for a long night.

Clutching my champagne flute with the same ardor with which I clutch my cell phone at parties in New York where I don't know anyone, I took gulp after gulp, and thought about my trip. The cashier who gave me incorrect change at the *boulangerie,* and the woman in line behind me who came to my defense. The cab driver who gave me his umbrella when I didn't have one. My mother's friend's husband, who told me that if I lived in France, there'd be a line of guys down the block waiting to date me. I wondered if that was true, or if I would move to France only to be just as doggedly single as I was in the United States. And was I single because I reveled in my independence, because I enjoyed living for myself, and only myself? Or was I single because I'd adapted it as a post-collegiate way of life, the way some people take up objectivism, or religion? I hailed the waitress and ordered a glass of red wine.

A new couple took their place at the other table next to mine, an Italian husband and wife who looked to be in their midforties. Out of the corner of my eye, I saw them sneaking glances at me as I stared intently ahead, resolving not to break down and take out my cell phone, so that at the very least I could scroll through my contacts in an effort to look busy.

I was now flanked by couples close enough that I wouldn't even have to extend my arm the entire way to reach for their salt. Given that there was nothing for me to do or anyone for me to talk to in order to fill my own silences, it became apparent, first to me, and then, in succession, to the couples on my left and right, that I would be serving as silent witness to their dinner. Not having heard me speak, they had no way of knowing my nationality—I could feel them consciously decide to be circumspect in conversation with each other. On my own, in France, and yet still somehow a fifth wheel.

Just when my dining anxiety was reaching alarming levels (I was either going to get drunk on red wine or fake an emergency and leave without eating, I had decided), my food arrived. Thinly sliced steak cooked *"bien cuit"* (which my guidebook had warned me was a temperature requested strictly by foreigners, but what can you do), a heaping portion of crispy fries that would make any other soggy iteration ashamed to call themselves French, and all of it doused in a sauce that—well, frankly, it looked green. Buttery, yes, but decidedly green, and nothing like the *au poivre* or A1 sauces I was used to being served in America.

I took a bite and—let me stop here to reiterate that I am not a foodie. My taste is lowbrow, my palate unrefined, my vocabulary for gastronomic delights, limited. I can't tell you what that first bite of steak and sauce tasted like—but I will say that I liked it so much I *smiled*. I smiled, goofily, happily, while dining alone in Paris, and I didn't care if the entire restaurant, the entire city, saw me.

I tucked in to that plate of *steak frites*: elbows out, neck low, right hand mechanically shoveling every last bite into my mouth as the Italian woman eyed me uncomfortably. And when the waitress came over to offer a second serving (seconds! At a restaurant! For free!), I helpfully thrust my plate toward her and let her pile it high with more frites than one human should be physically capable of eating. But eat them, I did. It was easy. They were that good.

And then, my plate was empty. I sat back, wiped my mouth with my napkin, and, sated, was finally able to sit in the restaurant without any of the anxiety or awkwardness that had plagued me not twenty minutes earlier. Poor Éponine, miserably wandering the streets by herself. If only she had been able to step in from the rain to eat a good steak and have a nice glass of wine! Then maybe she, by the fifth or sixth bite, would have come to the conclusion that there are worse fates in the world than being On Your Own in Paris. A waitress came by and asked if I wanted dessert. I demurred: it had been a great meal, and I didn't need the crème *brûlée* to perfect the experience. So I paid my bill and left, nodding courteously to the Italians, murmuring "Happy New Year" to the French.

On my walk home—and this time, I knew where I was going— I felt cheery, well fed, and happy to be spending a brisk January night in the Latin Quarter, with myself for company. And I remembered a conversation I'd had with my grandmother back in November, when I told her I wouldn't be coming home for Christmas. She described to me her first-ever trip to Europe, when she was forty years old. My grandfather was attending a conference, so she decided to use the opportunity to do the one thing she'd never done: travel. He went to sessions and she wandered around from country to country—her first time being off US soil, her first time leaving her three children at home for such an extended period. She told me about being in Italy and taking a taxi up Mount Etna. The driver was smoking and singing at the top of his lungs while maniacally rounding hairpin turns, while my grandmother clutched her seat belt and tried not to look at sheer drop after sheer drop. "And I thought to myself," she told me, *"I'm going to die! I'm going to die, and no one is ever going to know how happy I was."*

I was lonely in Paris (a little). But if someone had walked by me that night, on my way back to the little apartment after dining on *steak frites* and wine, smushed between two couples—if someone had walked by me and seen a girl on her own with an iPhone in one hand and a map of Paris in the other—they would have no way of knowing how happy I was.

LONDON: REAL CITY

Nicole Cliffe

During the summer of 2003, just after my sophomore year of college, I spent a summer living in London while writing for a budget travel guide. That it meant anything at all to me developmentally is relatively silly; London is one of the cushiest gigs you can get as a budget travel writer. There isn't a rampant culture of extortion or government corruption (depending on how you feel about the MPs' expenses scandal or *The Sun* or Jimmy Savile, naturally), you already speak the language, and the public transit system is so sufficiently snazzy that there are hundreds of blogs devoted to its observation and worship. You already know you're going to be able to drag out Samuel Johnson's "if a man is tired of London, he is tired of life" in your general introduction. Moreover, in 2003 the Internet was important, but not yet so important that people weren't buying physical budget travel guides. It was also a time in which narcissism demanded that I keep an elaborate, showy, expletive-laden diary and send it to my friends and family, but not a time in which that narcissism was so complete as to necessitate that I blog about the experience. *We had everything before us, we had nothing before us, we were all going direct to heaven, we were all going direct the other way*—or such are the literary allusions with which I peppered my unbearable reflections at the time.

I was Canadian, going into it, though attending college in the States, and the possessor of an Anglophilia that verged on the unpleasant. By which I mean to say that an actual English person, were they to grasp the extent of my Anglophilia, would be made uncomfortable by it and feel rather like the Rosetta stone when ringed by a group of pushy German tourists holding everyone else back with their arms. Generally, when one is Canadian, it's easy to downplay your Anglophilic obsessions to Americans with "Oh, you know, this is just what it's like when you grew up in the Commonwealth," but should there be another stealth Commonwealther in the room, they know you are lying. Canadians likely think more about the UK than Americans do (i.e., at times other than the Olympics or during royal weddings), but it is not, in fact, common to care anywhere near as much as I do—and certainly not as much as I did then.

The rising popularity of BBC America has made Anglophilia more socially acceptable; you can be noisy about *Doctor Who* or *Sherlock* or *Parade's End* without looking like a complete weirdo, although it is possible that only a complete weirdo would think that watching and talking about *Doctor Who* with any regularity makes you less than a complete weirdo. But then, of course, a true obsessive—like my father, who shuddered when Ken Burns launched *Jazz*—does not want too much company. There are ways in which *Downton Abbey* ruined Anglophilia. If you have *Tatler* sent to you monthly in a black plastic wrapper at great expense from overseas, you are not going to take fondly to people "discovering" Maggie Smith, as though she emerged fully formed and seventy years old from the head of Julian Fellowes.

I did not do a great job with my travel guide. Which is typical, I think, for things one does with the primary intention of having a

Transformative Emotional Experience through them, as well as for most travel guides written by twenty-year-olds. I was reasonably diligent, of course. Unlike some of my contemporaries, who swiftly learned that your daily allowance was not nearly enough to eat at every single one of the restaurants you were supposed to review, I dipped only a handful of times into the "recommend something that looks good on the takeout menu, collar people leaving restaurant to ask if they enjoyed their meal and would mind telling you what they ate, scribble obviously on a pad of paper while eating in hopes the restaurant will correctly assume you are reviewing them and take 40 percent off the bill" bag of unprofessional tricks. Nothing undermines your resolve to do a really good job more than arriving to fact-check a location from the previous year's edition and discovering that it hasn't been there for six years, or that it's across the street from what the map says, or that the suicide hotline in your emergency section is actually a takeaway.

The tenor of my experience of London was largely set at the introductory meeting, when I met the two other young women assigned to cover the city that summer and discovered they were both frail, painfully cool Asian women who actually understood what house music was. Since I looked more capable of drinking ale, and probably was, I was given the pubs beat and the museums beat and the old things beat, while they were given the responsibility of discovering what actual young people who lived in the city might enjoy doing. (Not looking at churches, not taking the day trip to Richmond while rereading *The Diary of a Nobody*, not trying to find 84 Charing Cross Road [it's not there].) They were lovely women, and I never saw them again. Our paths never crossed. We were never in the same London, and theirs was likely closer to the True London than mine, if there is such a thing.

When reading back over my diaries from the time (saved carefully by my mother, the only person other than me who could possibly care about my callow attempts at *explaining London*, as though a twenty-year-old kid who lived in a bedsit in Kensal Green for three months could be said to know anything whatsoever about London), I realized they're both better than I'd hoped and worse than I'd feared. They're funny, but the funniness is the funniness of Adrian Mole or Mr. Pooter (of the aforementioned *Diary of a Nobody*). The jokes are on the writer, always. I am the joke. I am not as funny as I think I am. The jokes I'm making right now in this piece will not seem funny to me when I am fifty, probably. I'll look at them like I look at those diaries: cringing, slightly, but with recognition. They're full of pop culture references and ALL CAPS and *motherfucker*s and complaints and poetic flourishes. They are the diaries of a person who, four months later, will read *Infinite Jest* for the first time and sink to her knees in despair. Someone who is not a virgin, but who has not yet been in love.

May 19, 2003 (Holborn)

Sir John Soane's Museum was extraordinary—he was an architect, and he stuck an awe-inspiring number of oddities into three combined houses in Lincoln's Field Rd. In addition to Hogarth's The Rake's Progress, *and a beautiful sarcophagus that he outbid the British Museum itself for in the early 19th century, Sir John collected all number of strange and interesting objects. So interesting is the museum, in fact, that my paces were dogged at all times by a BBC crew currently filming a documentary special on it. The commentator, Roland Something, was intensely posh and extremely nattily dressed and bumped into me three separate times.*

I can't swear to it, but I think I made that up. In my own diary! I am almost certain it did not happen. It's a perfect museum—that part is completely true—but I suspect that I was simply asked to wait briefly before entering a room so that a camera crew could get their shot, and then we moved on, our paths uncrossed and undogged. Things could be better than they are, so they must be made to fit. I can almost picture the imagined Roland Something (Why Roland? Why would that sound believable? Did I think I was writing a Martin Amis novel?).

May 20, 2003 (Holborn)

The absolute worst, worst sight in London was next on my list. I had seen various homages to Samuel Johnson all over Holborn; he and Pepys were everywhere. Therefore, I fondly assumed that "Dr. Johnson's House" would be interesting, or at least impressive. I was dead wrong. It was awful. It talks at great length about the heavily blacked-in books from which Dr. Johnson chose the words for his dictionary. Are they there? No. But we have facsimiles of later editions of the books, without Dr. Johnson's underlining. It talks about Dr. Johnson's voluminous personal correspondence. Are the letters there? No. But we have facsimiles of letters his sister wrote her friends. It talks about Dr. Johnson's extensive personal library. Oh, are these his books? No. But we have many books ABOUT Dr. Johnson. What else, if I may ask, does the museum have? Every portrait of Dr. Johnson ever done. And three copies of the 2002 Oxford English Dictionary. I will never watch the Blackadder *episode with the guy from* Cracker *the same way again.*

For some reason—likely that I was an idiot and just wanted to imitate Bill Bryson—I chose not to share the most perfectly Londonesque experience that Holborn offered me. I had not known, having mostly not emerged from a library and had a conversation until I was twenty-three, that Pepys was pronounced *Peeps,* as opposed to *Peppy's.* And so I said "Peppy's" to a stranger while getting directions, and he said, "Oh dear, make sure you remember it's

Peeps, or people will make fun of you." So, as an experiment, I said it incorrectly a few more times to different people, each of whom corrected my pronunciation nicely and cautioned me against future error, lest other Londoners become incensed with me. Because Londoners are like that, a little bit. They think they are a city of ogres, when in fact they are just people aware of human frailty like everyone else. They didn't want me to sound silly, but they weren't angry about it. People usually aren't.

May 21, 2003 (Holborn)
When I got back to my hostel, I was delighted to see that a large tour group of irritating high school students from America had just arrived, so I used my best fake accent and took off. I don't bother elaborately faking conversations with Londoners, it's pointless to try. I have, however, mastered a few stock phrases. So far, I possess a perfectly passable: "Do you have the time?" "Alright." "Sorry." "Excuse me." "Lovely." Of course, then you're fucked if they want to keep talking, because they'll sniff you out immediately.

Again, a lie. I spoke in a fake accent the *entire* summer, constantly, without stopping once. It was glorious. It also ruined my one chance to get lucky that summer, as I had been flirting mildly with a cute guy in a record store who was willing to open and play a John Renbourn CD for me (me, always on the cutting edge of popular culture) while I merrily chirped along, pretending to be a local, and when I got home and opened the jewel case, he had given me his number. Which I never called because I didn't have a phone and he would have asked me where I was from and what I was doing, and I would have had to reveal I was not actually a Londoner. When you're at a time in your life when embarrassment is the worst thing you can imagine, that's the kind of stupid decision you make. If I could go back, I'd call him and explain and we would laugh, because it was funny. Instead, I just cringed for a few weeks whenever I went near that neighborhood and worried he thought I didn't like him.

May 22, 2003 (Holborn)

I am writing this from the comfort of my own room, having moved into my bedsit. On a related note, I will be living an Oliver Twist existence until I get reimbursed for the two hundred and fifty quid deposit and/ or the two weeks rent I had to front. I think I have about a hundred dollars to eat and Underground with for the next week and a half, unless they hurry up. If I were eating on my own behalf, I'd be fine. Sixty-five pounds or so could keep me in Ritz crackers for at least a year, even if this is a city where waiters do not blink to charge you a pound for an eight-oz glass of lukewarm tap water. However, I'm supposed to be reviewing restaurants! I stole a towel from the shelf in my hostel today on my way out the door.

I've never stolen a thing in my life. And I said "quid." I said everything colloquial I could possibly say. "Rubbish," etc. If a planned sentence did not have a Britishism in it, a new sentence would be found. Two years later, in a fiction workshop, I would be unkind and pointed in my criticism of another student's short story that made the same mistake. For my sins, Joe, not yours.

May 26, 2003 (Bloomsbury)

What's up with public bathrooms in the UK? No one has paper towels. This is a nation of air dryers. I hate those things. Plus, the sinks have a hot faucet and a cold faucet. Pardon me—a scalding faucet, which immediately steams, and a freezing faucet, which turns your fingernails blue. The only exception I've seen is in McDonald's. No, I was not eating there. I had spilled coffee on myself on Kensington High Street and was VAINLY LOOKING FOR PAPER TOWELS.

To think that the worst thing that could befall you in a public bathroom in a foreign country is an absence of paper towels is a remarkable achievement. To be fair to my dippy younger self, recent studies have demonstrated that air dryers, despite their claims, are far less hygienic than paper towels, and as anyone could tell you, air dryers do not actually dry your hands—and wet hands are a better environment for germs. The more you know!

June 12, 2003 (Oxford)

Inside Tom Quad we saw the chestnut tree where Dodgson used to see the dean's cat sitting (his inspiration for both Dinah and the Cheshire Cat), and peeked into the dining hall which was so memorably transformed into Hogwarts.

The best part, though, was visiting Magdalen College. I have never seen anything so lovely in my entire life. Kevin and I were in shock. It was late afternoon, the choir was practicing in their chapel, and the light was doing beautiful things to the stonework. We went for a walk on the grounds, past their deer park (there are fawns! cavorting on the lawn!). There is a small, clear river that flows through the college's fields, and we could see a surprising number of fish darting about. The paths wind around through acres of woods and meadows, with little bridges and tiny benches, and the occasional fountain buried in the trees. By the time we were done prowling around, it was almost dark, and neither of us felt capable of talking.

Needless to say, we both picked up the Graduate Prospectus before leaving the city the next morning, after paying a visit to the shop where Alice Liddell used to buy her barley-sugar sweets (we bought barley-sugar sweets) and trying unsuccessfully to get into the botanical gardens, which were closed for no apparent reason.

That is the day I remember most clearly of all, mainly because my visiting friend Kevin and I literally sat in the grass and wept because it was so beautiful, and at that time we had so many out-sized emotions, which we had difficulty controlling. I recall being immeasurably sad because I wasn't an undergraduate there, preferably in the previous century, and then Kevin and I talked unbearably about *Brideshead Revisited* and *Death in Venice* for several hours and got ourselves some dinner. I remember it, too, because we were both so convinced we would come back to Oxford as graduate students, though neither of us did. I chose not to go to graduate school at all, a decision I am utterly at peace with, at least consciously. My only doubts stem from the fact that, at least once a month, I have a dream in which I suddenly panic because I did not go to graduate school—and so have lost touch with the professors who would have written recommendation letters for me—and then I wake up, terrified. And each time I ask myself if I really do wish I had gone to graduate school, but the answer remains no, and I go back to sleep.

June 28, 2003 (The City and East London)

Two weeks ago, I had almost finished the City, and just needed to type the whole thing up and mail it off before starting East London. Suddenly, my company laptop makes a hideous, awful grinding noise and dies. It's gone. I called my editor, and he promised to overnight me a new one.

In the meantime, I figured I would just finish my researching, maybe start East London early, type them both up when the replacement arrived and mail them together. With this plan in mind, I woke up early the next morning and went into the City. I fixed last year's map of the Temple, and realized I should probably eat at and review my last restaurant.

It was then that I made my fatal error. It occurred to me that my rent was due in two days and that my Travelcard was about to expire. Therefore, I hied myself to the nearest ATM and asked for a sum of money which was more than covered by the amount in my checking account.

My request was processed, and a *Counting Your Cash* message was flashed. Suddenly, this was replaced by *TRANSACTION CANCELLED*. I shrug, and reach out for my card. Which is not returned to me. Stupidly, I assume I must have idly returned it to my wallet. No. Sticking out of the machine? No. Wallet? No. Ground? No. Bowels of the NatWest on Fleet St? Yes.

I managed to briefly keep my cool at the bank until I got to speak to the manager, a man of deep and pervasive evil.

Me—"I'm terribly sorry to trouble you, but your cashpoint ate my card, and I need you to unlock the vestibule and get it for me."

Manager—"No, no. It is not here. It has . . . been sent."

Me—"You don't understand. This just happened. I don't care about the electronic idea of my card; I want the physical piece of plastic."

Manager—"No, no. It has been destroyed."

Me—"You said it has been 'sent.'"

Manager (smiles happily)—"No, no. The electronic idea of your card has been sent. The physical piece of plastic has been destroyed."

Long story short, after many many calls, my American bank promised to get me a new card for Monday (this was Thursday), and I had exactly six pounds left until then, no Travelcard for the tube, and when I got home that night, my new laptop was there, also broken. In reality, my bank card and my laptop didn't arrive until Friday, and I was under siege during business hours during that entire week hoping the laptop would arrive and I could sign for it. I ran out of books, I couldn't afford to go anywhere to buy internet time. I read The Lord of the Rings *in French* (Frodon Sacquet et l'Anneau unique), *I read* Crime and Punishment, *I read* Orlando, *I read* Birthday Letters, *I read the complete Rimbaud, and I even read an extensive newsletter from a cosmetics company. I smoked my last pack of Silk Cut. I literally ate *nothing at all except for a pack of biscuits someone had left in my bed-sit's kitchen and a can of salmon. Each day, once my packages failed to arrive yet again, I walked all the way from Kensal Green into the city center, and then back, like a vampire, under shade of night. But now all is well.*

I was smoking Silk Cut cigarettes, which are disgusting. They are disgusting, and they are the cigarette smoked by Detective Inspector Frost in R. D. Wingfield's A Touch of Frost series of crime novels, later adapted for the screen and starring David Jason. If I could have any job in the world, any job at all, and live my entire life doing that job, I would want to be a detective for the Thames Valley CID. It's what I've spent the most time preparing to do, to the extent that reading prepares one for things, and it appeals to me more than anything else. And the image I have of a person doing that job is a crumpled, poorly dressed me, leaning against a stone wall next to a dead body, trying not to flick Silk Cut ash onto it, and drinking a mug of tea that a constable has handed me.

I read so many great things that summer. I read all of Philip Larkin, all of Ted Hughes. I read *A Dance to the Music of Time*. Paul Celan. *Mrs. Dalloway*. Paul Monette's *Love Alone: Eighteen Elegies for Rog*. *The Child in Time*. *The Road to Wigan Pier*. Claire Messud's *The Hunters*. It may have been the last great summer for me of reading physical book after physical book. I read books, and I thought about the one I wanted to write. I picked the right epigraph for it, from John Ashbery's "As One Put Drunk into the Packet-Boat":

Down there, for a moment, I thought
The great, formal affair was beginning, orchestrated,
Its colors concentrated in a glance, a ballade
That takes in the whole world, now, but lightly,
Still lightly, but with wide authority and tact.

I don't still think I really have a novel to write, but I did then. It was good for me to think that, because I read like a person who was apprenticing to write a novel and wanted to learn from the best. And, too, when inconvenient or distressing things happened to me like the aforementioned logistical calamities, or my landlord withholding my deposit unless I went out with him, or just being very, very lonely (with my fake accent), it seemed wonderful, because it was all copy.

June 29, 2003 (East London)
The Whitechapel Gallery, which I saw next, was one of the major highlights of the neighborhood for me. There was a major retrospective of the work of one of my favourite photographers, Philip-Lorca diCorcia, and it was breathtaking. In addition, I saw a couple of really interesting video pieces, and an amazing sound installation. I love that such a fantastic cultural hub is sitting in one of London's slummiest neighbourhoods. And it's popular, which always gives me faith in humanity.

Oof. Art for the poor, guv'nor? Moreover, I do not know, now, who Philip-Lorca diCorcia is, and I probably didn't know then, either.

I do not regret the awfulness of these diaries, which are quickly represented in the snippets here. If anything, I mildly relish it. And I love having had these memories returned to me. What I do regret, I think—and please keep in mind that I am not sure even of this point—is the time I must have spent writing them. The difficulty in internalizing that regret, of course, is that all I do now is write about things that are happening, as I did then, and I have clearly made a bargain with myself that this state of affairs is acceptable to me and a decent way to live one's life. It's my job, and I enjoy it. When painted in stark relief, however, the reality is that I was twenty and living in London and free of husbands and children and work and mortgages and yet chose to spend several hours a week hunched over in an Internet café trying to make jokes about how terrible sandwiches are in the UK. That *must* have been a mistake, for me. I don't regret buying so many books I couldn't afford that I needed to acquire a new cheap suitcase at a Sainsbury's in order to lug them home. I still use the suitcase, and I only paid fifteen pounds for it. My father, who has not held a job in many decades, due to being magically charming enough to find women to support him, once told me: "You will never remember the money you saved by having a shitty meal or staying in a bad hotel room," and I think this can be extended to book purchasing. But the time! The time, I do regret. I should have gone on dates. I should have gone out, even once, instead of taking long baths every night and thinking about how I would finally be ready to be a woman when I returned home.

But this is the thing about youth that people get wrong, she says fatuously from her great age of thirty. We like to think that it's wasted on the young, which is a profound untruth. Youth would be wasted on the not-young, and the examined life is the only one really worth living. The reason you can spend your evenings eating a pasty in the tub while reading Ted Hughes at twenty and enjoy it is because you don't understand that you're going to be hemmed in by life, eventually. You do it not knowing emotionally (most nonmorons do know it intellectually) that there are a limited number of days in your life when you will have the great privilege of being bored and self-indulgent. That the great joy of being young is not taking it seriously, not trying to make every minute count, not thinking about how you'll never be twenty years old and completely free ever again. Were we to get a do-over, we might make better choices, but that perfect carelessness and apathy would be gone. You can't go home again, etc.

I'm going back to London next spring for an extremely belated (the first kid will be potty trained by then) honeymoon. I have some money now, and a perfect well-researched ten-day itinerary, and friends to visit, and I'm very excited. I may finally sit in a black cab, which at the time seemed financially similar to paying the Russians to take you into space with them, and eat at a restaurant with cloth napkins, and buy postcards. But I'm already picturing a clearer London, with more defined edges. London is one of the world's great cities. It exists, it works, it's overpriced, and the real estate market is being cornered by oligarchs. Boris Johnson is the *mayor* now. When I was there, he was writing op-eds about how his driver's license had been taken away as a result of the new speed cameras.

I just finished the rock journalist Rob Sheffield's new book, *Turn Around Bright Eyes: The Rituals of Love and Karaoke,* and he says: "Your Beatles will change all through your life." (He's correct.) I would end this with: "Your London will change all through your life," but perhaps the difference between twenty and thirty is knowing that London is not a metaphor, and that cities are unique and functioning bureaucratic systems and centers of commerce that do not exist to show you who you are, or tell you who you will become. London is very, very old, and London doesn't give a shit. But, at twenty, you don't know that yet, and that is why you might long to be twenty again, even though it would be utterly and completely wasted on you, the no-longer-truly-young.

HOW TO TRAVEL

Jim Behrle

I'm not entirely sure I like to travel. But I do like having traveled. And I like thinking about future travel. But the actual traveling makes me feel anxious, displaced, turned around. Waking up in a different bed, especially a hotel bed, makes me feel for a few minutes like maybe I've died, that purgatory really does exist, and that I'm there. Maybe I should invent glasses that I could wear to bed so that, upon waking, my surroundings would look just like my bedroom at home. And I wouldn't feel so immediately out of joint. Although at some point I would still have to take those glasses off and realize I was in a La Quinta in Fresno, surrounded by bags of yesterday's In-N-Out Burger. But if half the fun of travel is getting there, then half the antifun of travel is worrying about how to get back.

Not that home is the Trump Tower for me or anything. It's simply the place I don't have to worry about getting home from. Which subway will I take? I don't have to, I'm already here. I used to sleep in a hammock in a basement at one point, and I considered that home. "Oh, man, I'm so glad to be in my hammock in the basement!" What's the magic that this idea of home holds over us?

And why are we always trying to escape it on some kind of vacation? If you told me, a younger me, years ago, that I would call New Jersey home someday, that younger me would have laughed in your face. It's part of the conversation I imagine having with myself in case I ever truly perfect time travel. "You're forty? You don't have a girlfriend? Or a dog? Or a car? And you live in New Jersey? And you never got to play point guard for the Celtics?" The conversation gets more absurd as the years pass, and I don't even have cool facial hair anymore.

Why do I always feel like I'm headed in the wrong direction? I'll be sitting with a boarding pass at gate 21 at 7:30 a.m., waiting for an 8:30 a.m. flight to Pittsburgh. I'll check my ticket at least a half-dozen times. Am I really headed to Pittsburgh? Yes; I have Pirates tickets in my other pocket. Does it really say gate 21, or does it say gate 2.1? I guess there is no dot there; it looks more like a comma. Is this really a JetBlue counter? Probably; they are wearing blue kerchiefs. And on it goes, the terrible spin cycle that my brain always seems to be on.

If I think I'm in the right place, though, I'm generally in the wrong place. This is maybe a result of the first intercontinental trip I ever took. I was a young future-exchange student headed to Germany, the French were having an air strike, and one day all flights to Paris from the United States were canceled. We stayed in a hotel near JFK and watched a documentary on transvestites. Perhaps New York cable had a channel that was all transvestites back then? It was a long documentary. And we couldn't sleep. We flew to Paris the next morning, only to find that all flights to Germany from there had also been canceled. So we hung out in a closed Charles de Gaulle for a day, with little to eat, and at one point I was wearing a bathrobe with a Sabena airlines miniblanket tied around my head. Still without sleep, we took a delirious ride through Paris on a bus the next morning, and then took a long train ride to Munich. And this was what happened when I was in the exact right place doing exactly what I was supposed to do. With someone else, some benevolent force above, booking hotels with transvestite channels and planes with miniblankets. Imagine if it had been entirely up to me.

When Mrs. Dunbar asked us all in eighth grade what we wanted to be when we grew up, I wrote about wanting to be a travel agent. I don't remember exactly what it was about being a travel agent that initially interested me. Plastic palm trees, possibly? I don't think I ever truly wanted to be a travel agent at all. I just resented the question. "I'm twelve years old. Please let me live and not have to worry about being an adult." It's a question I still chafe at. Where do you see yourself in five years? Dating a robot, hopefully. But I wrote about wanting to be a travel agent. About wearing Hawaiian shirts to work. About how happy travel agents get to make their customers, who fly off to wonderful places with their help and come back with so many wonderful memories. I imagine the actual lives of travel agents to be a little more complicated than all that. And that their workdays frequently involve angry long-distance phone calls from Tajikistan. "But the Westin in Kulob says you never booked a suite for us!" I certainly don't think I'd want to handle the pressure of trying to plan someone else's happy memories for them, either. I didn't become a travel agent, thankfully. Especially thankful is that couple in Tajikistan.

But perhaps I can still help your travel dreams come true. By imparting upon you, gentle e-reader, some knowledge won from wearing Santa Claus suits through security checkpoints and drinking Moxie in Maine most summers. Let my anxiety work for you; let it wash over you and then come hurriedly boomeranging back to me, where it belongs. You need not travel worried. Let me do all the worrying for the both of us.

Whatever They're Eating, You Ought to Try It

We're not talking about eating monkey brains in an Indiana Jones movie here. But wouldn't you eat monkey brain once if everyone else was? Because even if it was seriously gross, you could always tell people something tasted like monkey brains. "This soufflé is worse than monkey brains. And I should know! You never really get the aftertaste of ganglia out of your mouth—so garlicky!" But every corner of the world has some kind of weird thing that you ought to try while you're in town. It could be the wrong color or made out of animals we don't normally eat. It's tough to be vegan and vegetarian on the road, though, but I'm sure there's some kind of moss or fern that's specific to wherever you're headed that they'll happily climb to a mountaintop to find for you. Offering food is a sign of good hospitality, and American travelers ought to take hospitality wherever they can get it, because 90 percent of the earth's population wants to feed us knuckle sandwiches most of the time. We ought to accept the monkey brains we get with a little grace and in the spirit of world friendship.

I had a sandwich filled with French fries in Pittsburgh. Why do they put French fries in the middle of sandwiches in Pittsburgh? You can google *Why do they put French fries in the middle of sandwiches in Pittsburgh?*—they've been doing it for a long time. And if restaurants have been doing something for longer than a month, it's a thing. A thing that has not killed anyone. A thing that enough people have ordered that it's still on the menu. And a thing you ought to try. Just so you can have a conversation with anyone from Pittsburgh for the rest of your life that begins "I've been to Pittsburgh. I like those sandwiches with the French fries inside."

Each American city seems to have a specific kind of food that only tourists eat. So what? Embrace your inner tourist! I spent my time in Munich wandering around without a map or a guide. I saw the same French movie twice. It was called *A World Without Pity.* Why did I see it twice? Because I was going in circles. Because I refused to look at a map. Because I didn't want anyone to know I was an ugly American tourist. Which they probably already knew, because I was walking in circles and watching the same bad French movie over and over again. Although the couple in the movie, despite being separated, did do this cool thing where they could snap their fingers and the lights on the Eiffel Tower would go off. That was a good trick. That would probably get you thrown in Gitmo today, but the '90s were a gentler age, all tattoos and grunge music.

Definitely drink whatever they're drinking. In Prague, this meant, between pints, a tiny horrible green drink called Becherovka. It is, possibly, just a weird trick drink they're playing on tourists. Like the first time someone introduces you to wasabi and makes you take a giant faceful of it. But the Becherovka made it so that I don't remember much of my time in the great city of Prague. It gave me a foggy dreamfulness, and a floating feeling that nothing there could ever hurt me. I was even struck by a streetcar—nothing. That was the Becherovka at work. A green haze fixed upon me. I was a ghost and also a person pretending to be a ghost. It was an experience definitely worth allegedly having. Like a character in some kind of Ivan Klíma novel, I was pulled between the sadness of the waking world and the erotic pulsings of a never-ending dreamscape. No, it was like a Chagall painting. I was holding my own hand and the other me was floating away like a magic bride.

The bottle I brought back to the United States with me almost got confiscated, but I could never rekindle the passion I once felt for the Becherovka. We grew apart. I stayed out all hours of the night, hoping it would go to bed before I got home, but it would stay there on the counter, mocking me. It was a love affair worth having, though, as most love affairs are. Just typing the word *Becherovka* still reminds me of its bitter green kiss. I am going into the other room to sob uncontrollably now.

Moxie soda is the trick I play on myself each summer up at the campground my friends let us visit each July. It tastes like molasses sneezed right at you. But I wanted to become a better New Englander. I wanted to feel the roots of my people as they spread through the great frozen land beneath our Red Sox–cheering feet. I wanted to be one of those guys who like drinking Moxie soda. There's a guy pointing right at you on its orange can, practically daring you to drink it. Are you daring me, little pointing man? Well, I'll show you! Glug glug glug. Hmmm.

Ted Williams did their ads back in the day. And even though he was from San Diego, he represents some kind of ultra-grumpy New Englander in my mind. No ten feet of snow is going to stop Ted from candlepin bowling today! He refused to hit to left field when teams would move all their infielders to the right side of the baseball diamond. Why? He thought his meanness would overcome their gloves and positioning. He probably would have hit .500 if he just tapped it down the third-base line. But that is not the way of the New Englander. They are a proud, stubborn, indefatigable people who don't say hello on the street. They used to make kids go to school when there was, like, five inches of snow on the ground. To toughen them up. Like the Starks of Winterfell in *Game of Thrones*, every New Englander once imagined himself or herself a hale and hearty winter-proof warrior. Put the chains on the wheels, fire up the blowtorches. Someday you might have to make clam chowder out of just rocks and a little Moxie soda. So get yourself ready. In New England, Winter isn't just Coming, it is usually there. Six straight months of sunless despair. Surrounded by snowbanks the size of stegosauruses.

That's what drinking Moxie soda means to me. Accepting that if you drink enough bitterness in life, it starts to taste sweet to you. Not unlike Conan O'Brien drinking his own tears. And then the tears making him stronger. He is also a New Englander. Does he like Moxie? Probably not. They only really sell it in New Hampshire and Maine. But there, it's everywhere. I still intend to buy the house with the big bottle of Moxie coming out of it that's also a roadside attraction in Union, Maine, if you're ever traveling through there. I will buy that house as soon as I have some money.

Maybe if Moxie was called Wuss Juice, I wouldn't like it so much. *Wuss Juice* does have a certain ring to it, though. If marketed correctly. But like all weird regional sandwiches and drinks, Moxie requires courage of a certain sense. Not like hard-won courage, more like drunken campsite courage. The kind that makes you try the hot wings at Duff's in Buffalo, New York. Or the Burrito As Big As Your Head in Chicago. These experiences, even more than going to the big reflecting bean or the famous waterfall, will stay with you. I think I am still digesting those hot wings. The stomach never forgets. And now Moxie soda tastes like summer to me. And I am a little better for that. Only a little. But a little.

Plan Ahead but Then Break All Your Plans

Once upon a time, as a gift for not drinking alcohol for six months, I planned a little vacation for myself. I bought a weeklong pass on the Greyhound bus and found six cities with baseball parks I wanted to visit in six days: Detroit, Chicago, Cincinnati, Saint Louis, Kansas City, and Pittsburgh. I'd given myself staycations before, going to multiple Red Sox games over the course of a week. That's much more difficult now, to score the same seats over four consecutive nights in July at Fenway Park, but it was a different, if not better, world back then. I didn't check my cell phone once in the stands. Because cell phones didn't exist. I would have had some great tweets about the flash-in-the-pan phenomenon named Midre Cummings, who seemed to be having the week of his life in the Majors that week, though. But the most interesting things to me were the rhythms of a baseball game, and how they repeated themselves day after day. They play the same songs between innings. In a certain inning, a guy on the edge of the bleachers will get drunk enough to try to start the wave. He will enlist his friends. Everyone will start getting bossy. It's like standing over a grill and trying to figure out with your pals how to ignite the coals. But the fans want to do the wave. I do not want to do the wave; I just want to see how the wave gets done, day after day. It is not something I knew I wanted to know. But that is the wonder of travel, even when you're on a staycation. What will you discover about the place you already know everything about?

Anyway, could I attend six baseball games in six nights? I didn't have the money to stay in hotels, so the trip required me to know someone in each of the towns I was visiting. But this was the beginning of the age of the Internet, and the early days of poetry blogging, so I basically knew someone everywhere. Those people possibly wanted to punch me in the face, but that didn't mean they wouldn't let me crash on their couch after punching me. I didn't know anyone in Chicago, though, but how hard is it to befriend someone in Chicago and get invited back to their place? I'm sure White Sox fans do that kind of thing all the time—take in stranger Red Sox fans and give them a couch to sleep on. And one of those hot dogs covered in every vegetable imaginable. I'd deal with Chicago when I got to Chicago. And if I needed to sleep in a Chicago bus station or on a weird overnight bus to Saint Louis, well, OK. I've slept in apartments with bedbugs, how bad could a bus station be? Maybe it's worse, because there's just one Big Bedbug. Who eats burritos the size of your head?

The danger of me planning a trip is that I can sit behind a computer and be, like, "Eight hours on a bus every day for a week? No problem." The Internet distends all reality into unthinkable madness. But at least I had lots of books to read. And the A.A. *Big Book*, which is like twenty books rolled all into one. Plus I was sure that what I would discover out the window of a Greyhound along my adventure into America's spleens would also be profoundly exciting. Had I ever truly seen a cornfield? Maybe in a movie like *Field of Dreams*. But what mad truth could I glean from hours and hours of staring at, say, Taco Bells and Porn-and-Fireworks shops out the window between Saint Louis and Kansas City? And then back the same damn way? I would find that out, and that knowledge would be something I would take with me evermore. That movie is about getting rid of cornfields and letting the baseball fields out, by the way. Also unknowable at the time of the Internet booking: what the weather might be like across our great land the last week in August. Would I roll right into six straight rainouts in six different cities? Very possibly. But no. Would I contract prairie madness? Because that would suck.

The first lesson of the bus is that the bus is always late. Late pulling into huge traffic into Detroit. We actually broke down outside Saint Louis, me and a busful of Amish people. Apparently they can ride buses; they just can't drive buses? The reaction of eighty Amish people on a broken-down bus is priceless. They're all looking at each other like, "Beats me how to fix it, I'm Amish. If this was a buggy, I could fix it in a second." We were late pulling into Cincinnati, and I was so late getting into Pittsburgh that I missed the game completely and my seven-day pass expired. I thought I was going to have to live in the Pittsburgh bus station for the rest of my life. Which, you know, it could be worse. I had planned everything rather well, even to the point of when things ran really late, it was no big deal. In New York when I'm late, everything seems terrible and overwhelming, and it feels like I'm always rushing and trying to overcome my lateness in some way. If only I'd planned better! But, I don't know, sometimes the bus just blows two tires. I'm more like the Amish guys than I thought. I couldn't fix the damn bus, either. And I can't control everything or foresee every outcome. If I could, chili dogs would be the healthiest thing in the world. And they'd be free, handed out on the street by dudes in mascot outfits.

I got to Detroit eventually, and I met up with someone I'd been in an Internet fight about poetry with. It's good, if you're going to travel all over willy-nilly, to be part of some weird online community. Knitters, master/slave BDSM groups. People who read *thehairpin. com*! Anything. Most people have couches. And there is just something about the intimacy of meeting people online that makes you want to discover them, let them crash on your couch, for some reason. I wouldn't let me crash on my couch, though. And I'd never felt the need to meet anyone I'd fought with on the Internet in person. Until her. Maybe it was because she was a woman. (Everyone on the Internet could be! Until they're not!) Maybe because we had both fought in those comment fields so bravely for two different sides. It seemed like a perfectly absurd idea to hang out with a complete stranger who liked THAT KIND OF POETRY. But I generally trust my own ability to charm my way through any awkward situation. Especially given eight hours on a bus to mentally prepare.

After placidly sitting quietly for eight hours, I am like a comedian on meth. It's a charm siege. I'm sure she felt charmed, and besieged. This rather wonderful poetry and rock 'n' roll lady living in Detroit, willing to go to a Tigers game with me. The thing you have to get used to in downtown Detroit, at least at that time, was the constant police sirens. There would be a cute bowling alley/record store next to a boarded-up building. Next to a flipped-over car. And she's just calmly showing me the sights as we walk up to where the Tigers and Lions play: "Over there they sell cupcakes. That is a vacant lot filled with feral kittens." It was like some kind of Mad Max, Post-Punk Fallujah. She was cool, and she was pretty, and she was tough. And I liked everything about her. And about Detroit. I have an affinity for fucked-up broken things. Because I am one.

It was hot in the cheap seats and the Tigers were awful then. The game went extra innings. She pointed to all the buildings in the Detroit skyline and how most of them were empty. Giant office buildings filled with offices nobody goes to. After the game was mercifully finished, we walked to the monorail. Yes, Detroit has a monorail. Does your city have a monorail? No? Then quit making fun of Detroit. It's called the People Mover. Which is kind of a great '70s-ish name, when you think about it. It used to run in a circle, but one side got burned-out or something, so it kind of loops up and back along the remaining C. We saw the casino in Chinatown, and the Canadian casino that mirrors it across the shimmering Great Lake. The People Mover kind of hums over everything, acts like something out of *Jurassic Park*. Here's a safe place to witness the spectacle of descent. How can whatever happened to Detroit, a grand American city, happen? Beats me. But the echoes of that grandness remain, Art Deco hotels with deteriorating exteriors, boarded-up windows. It was like taking a rowboat through a dead whale.

I had to leave early the next morning if I was to make it to Chicago. But I hadn't found any pals to crash with there, though, so there was no couch waiting for me. And the Cubs weren't even in town, so I had gotten White Sox tickets. The White Sox are nice and all, but watching a Cubs game is like watching Gargamel cook and eat the Smurfs. The ballpark is amazing; the fans are amazing. Is there a sports experience as strange and as wonderful as watching the home team get beat down in the midafternoon August sun and have their fans be Beckettian, cheerful and Midwestern about it? I don't know, because I still have never gotten to Wrigley Field. I had White Sox tickets. And the prospect of traveling for eight hours to meet no one and sleep nowhere seemed daunting. When here in Detroit, I could revel in the companionship of my Internet-fight friend. I could feel some sparks. Wouldn't sparks be better than sleeping on a bus all day?

So I stayed in Detroit and made out with my friend. It was wonderful high-school-era making out. We almost drowned in each other a couple of times. Breathing seemed of very little consequence. Kissing was the thing. And it went on and on.

It's a very happy memory, my trip to Detroit. Maybe the highlight of the baseball trip. Although eating Cincinnati chili is a very close second. Sometimes, with all my worrying and fretting about being late, being in the wrong place, is this the bus to France? I forget that I may in fact be in the right place at the right time doing the exact right thing.

The Hotel Is Usually the Best Part

Even more than I love crashing on people's couches and possibly making out with those people when I'm on the road, I love hotels. Who isn't a sucker for a room you'll never have to clean up?

The first thing I do when I check into a hotel is immediately trash the bed to suit my purposes. Which is sadly usually just sleeping. I can only afford hotels when someone else is affording it. Like Ben, who I live with, and just isn't a crash-on-the-couch kind of guy. So when we travel like a family, it's first class the whole way. No mattresses in the middle of the woods for us. I just wad up all the pillows, of which there are always millions. What are these pillows for? Toss them. I take their insane comforter, a giant puffy layer of fluffy nonsense, and pitch that across the room. I am marking my territory, like a wolverine probably does on some Nature Channel show I will never watch.

But there's the right hotel and then there's a just a hotel-hotel. I stayed in one of the worst hotels I've ever been to, in Buffalo, New York. Someone had clearly been murdered in the room I was staying in. Or maybe it would have just made the perfect setting for a murder. Bed rough and made much too tightly. I could envision a prostitute killing a trick in a room like that. Some insurance salesman who called him "pumpkin" just like his uncle used to . . . and then getting left in the hollowed-out box spring. Leaving a weird knee lump in the mattress. Which was right in my back. I checked under the mattress and there was no dead traveling salesman, but most likely they'd just gotten rid of the body. There was a Holiday Inn right across the parking lot. Somehow I had missed that as I'd searched the Internet. What I wouldn't have paid to be in a bland hotel that night, as I lay, sleepless and stiff as a board, upon the sheets of the recently murdered guy and enjoyed an entire night of teeth-chattering terror as I was visited by three ghosts. That is the only night of my life I would have rather stayed in a Holiday Inn.

La Quinta, on the other hand, is a great little hotel chain. Our room was rather cheap and charming. In Fresno, no less! It was a room I didn't feel bad about eating In-N-Out burgers in. A lot of

In-N-Out burgers. It was like a big comfy Converse Sneakers Box. For some reason, the bathroom door of practically every hotel I have ever stayed in either opens the wrong way or hits the sink at some weird angle. So there's lots of advice given while brushing teeth, and many parties are heard from during that whole process. Many opinions must be endured.

The first time I traveled to New York for business, my bookstore asked me which reasonably rated hotel I wanted to stay in. I chose the Chelsea Hotel, naturally. I knew it to be a place of rare beauty and terrible darkness, both sometimes inhabiting the same crazy space. Writers, singers, painters, junkies, Ramones, Ethan Hawkes. They all once called it home. It was totally worth staying there, whatever that bookstore paid. Spooky and haunted and crazy. There is clearly not a Chelsea Hotel in any other city. There is barely one in New York, anymore. But how do you find that balance between a unique experience and one in which there are bugs crawling all over everything? And you haven't even taken any acid yet?

I guess you just have to call around and google and stuff. I planned a trip for Ben and me once. The idea was to see Conan O'Brien on his I-Don't-Have-a Show-Anymore tour. I felt bad for Conan, and thought it would be fun to support him on this new wacky venture. But, by the time I actually got around to looking for tickets to one of the venues, there was only one in the country with tickets remaining. Reno, Nevada. I had never imagined I might want to visit Reno, or Nevada for that matter. I am not much of a gambler, and at that time I wasn't drinking. That takes two big reasons to go there off the board. Ben came home and I told him Reno was all that was left. We looked at a map. He told me how he'd always imagined traveling to Sequoia National Park in California. I said we could do both. Stay for a day or two in Reno, then wander down to Sequoia. Then Ben added Yosemite. But he didn't want to drive the whole way. So we could take a train. A magical train, apparently. The California Zephyr. It connects Chicago and San Francisco, and for our purposes Reno and Sacramento, across the Sierra Nevada mountains. Up past Donner Lake, across mountaintops still filled with snow in the early part of May, through all these weird little Gold Rush towns, back down to the state capital of California. Of course, I wanted to see some minor league baseball along the way. And *Iron Man 2* was coming out that particular weekend. So a plot got hatched.

Ben, for all his lovely qualities, doesn't like to do the detail work. He was willing to foot the bill, and I, unemployed bearded lump of glob, was to figure out all the specifics. But specifics and details and real life and the human condition are not my specialties, either. I live in a reverie of dreamworld nonsense. I am a poet. But I also spend most of my waking hours wondering what would happen if a sinister alien inhabited Lois Lane and made her into a villainess. What would Superman do? Would he call up Batman and be like, "You have to come beat up Lois Lane! I just can't do it! I love her so much! But she's robbed every bank in Metropolis. I have to go! I haven't broken up with her, either. She has this kryptonite-encrusted bedroom whip! Help!" My mind is a morass of almost constant distraction. So how could I, Idiot Boy, plan a thing that involved planes, trains, automobiles, and also, with a little luck, In-N-Out burgers?

The Internet, although very handy for most situations, came up surprisingly lame in some circumstances during all this. Although booking most stuff was relatively easy, booking it on the Internet can seem like watching the stars through a kaleidoscope. It's all very pretty, but you might not want to fly right into it. The reality of some situations is not clear from just a Google search. For example, we ended up wanting to fly out of San Francisco. Lovely town. Delightful people. Giants! Rice-A-Roni! Beat Poets! Hills! Trolleys! Vertigo! I recommend it. But Ben decided he wanted to stay at a certain hotel on a certain street. In most towns, streets are all kind of flat and walkable. In San Francisco, glaciers apparently built all of the streets at random and deposited them on the sides of crazy hills. Our hotel was on a crazy hill. I mean, crazy. At the very top. Like a ninety-five-degree sidewalk brings you there. Want some Starbucks. No problem, just fall down this hill and then get a Sherpa to carry you back to your hotel. Wonderful views of the city. Do I remember any of those wonderful views? No. I remember falling down the hill and having a few coronaries climbing back up. Just to get Starbucks coffee. Which is OK. But I really like the people who work in Starbucks. I want to date someone who works in Starbucks. I once had a grand Internet affair with someone who worked in a Starbucks in West Hollywood, and she had all these cool stories of celebrities, about which were nice and which were jerks and what they drank. And she was beautiful and probably smelled like coffee and probably wore one of those white Starbucks shirts with the little green visor and maybe a green apron. For me, for some reason, the Starbucks uniform is even better than the French maid uniform. Irène Jacob, from the movie *Red*—beautiful, wonderful actress— was in the second *Fugitive* movie called *U.S. Marshals*. She played Wesley Snipes's girlfriend who worked at Starbucks. And she had a cool French accent. For me, her performance is one of the most erotic ever set to film. All she does is, like, work at Starbucks and help Wesley Snipes escape Tommy Lee Jones. God bless you, Irène Jacob. And your Starbucks uniform!

So that hotel didn't work out so well. Neither did the one I booked at Mono Lake on the eastern side of Yosemite. Apparently not all the roads through the park are passable, even in early May.

Because of snow. Frigging snow. Great when falling, essential when skiing. But a pain in the ass the rest of the time. We would not be able to get through the park to beautiful Mono Lake. To stay in whatever cheap place I had found there. So we needed another place to stay near Visalia, California, for one more night. But the charming bungalow motel I found and booked at the entrance to Sequoia National Park (By the way, that place is amazing. And sequoias are just so regal, like really old giant people that don't move around anymore. Ben and I highly recommend it.) was full, so I asked the nice lady at the desk what we should do. She called a competitor down the way and got us a room. Very nice of her! It was a combo motel/farm/zoo of some kind? There was a donkey. A very loud donkey. You might think donkeys are tons of fun to be around, but there's just something so off-putting about that donkey-sound donkeys make. My goodness. It was the night Betty White hosted *Saturday Night Live*. And I could hear the donkey and only the donkey. His donkey call went straight into my soul. I fell asleep. I dreamed of donkeys. I was chased by donkeys.

The best hotel we stayed at was in Sacramento. I'd taken the time to, like, call the Sacramento Chamber of Commerce or something. Google was completely unhelpful when it came to Sacramento. I wanted a cool hotel. Something nice and not so expensive. The woman seemed puzzled. Maybe they don't get many tourists? I mean, there was an older, more touristy part of Sacramento we stayed in that had a cool Old West look to it. Just a few square blocks of Old Town that looked like a stagecoach might pull up. Which I kinda hoped would happen.

So where should we stay, Chamber of Commerce Lady? "Well, there is a hotel in an old riverboat." *Riverboat* you say? Sleeping upon the bubbling waves of the Sacramento River inside a riverboat that they turned into a hotel? Oh, yeah, we're definitely doing that!

I didn't even mind that the room was small. Or that the room was tipped. It was better than a water bed. We ate mango gelato on the deck facing out, the sun just going down. It was a quick walk to a minor league baseball park, where we watched about six innings of the Sacramento River Cats before we got bored and left. For my money, Sacramento is a magical place with a cool yellow bridge. We had spent the morning on the California Zephyr, with its Plexiglas ceilings, so you could take in the Sierras as they cut across the continent. Gone up past Donner Lake. The train had some kind of Train Expert speaking in soothing NPR tones over our entire morning voyage, letting us know just how much dynamite it took to carve this particular path through the mountains. And how many people died trying to lay track through this cold, rarefied air. It was a magical day! Train with plastic roof, stagecoach-ready Old Town, floating hotel. We downloaded the latest episode of the last season of *Lost* onto Ben's iPod and watched it on the bed as we bobbed along the river. A perfect day if I have ever had one. We used to really like *Lost*.

But Ben's favorite hotel was the Wawona. Inside Yosemite Park. It was also the most expensive. It's nestled beside a lonely, twisty road between the main famous part of the park and a more serene sequoia-dotted part. They had housed troops there or something at some point; it was a weird garrison-looking place. But the key to its charm were the creaky floorboards and a distinct lack of televisions. All hotel rooms should have televisions. Because you should definitely pick up a newspaper *and* watch the news wherever you go. (That's how we'd found out about the rodeo in Vasalia. Rodeo! While we were in town! We went! It was weird! But good weird. And the BBQ was good.) But there were no televisions because there hadn't been any televisions when they built the place, or something, and they'd wanted to maintain its original grace and charm, and apparently that meant no TVs. They had lights! They had a hair dryer, one of those terrible hotel ones you wouldn't want to use. Had Teddy Roosevelt once dried his hair with one of those? Also, they had no telephones. But no TVs? If TVs had existed back in the day, John Muir would definitely have had one in his room. Make no mistake. I don't think there was wi-fi, either, but you know, screw the Internet. I always want to go on the Internet to have fun, but it always turns into some kind of work.

But Ben loved this hotel. We spent a Mother's Day in the hail up there, eating meatloaf and taking in the rustic charm of it all. When we speak of the trip, he lets the word *Wawona* fall from his lips as if it were the most beautiful word ever invented. And I nod. And think of the old riverboat. I would like to live on an old riverboat someday. Floating on the Hudson. To get to work, I would tie it up someplace near the West Side Highway and walk to the bookstore. And then come back and we would float away! On the wonderful waves. Until Bloomberg banned that, too. Boo, Bloomberg, boo.

But my favorite hotel in all the land is the Commander Hotel in Cambridge, Massachusetts. I like the big red neon SHERATON COMMANDER sign that hangs atop it over Cambridge Common, beckoning. As it no doubt once beckoned General Washington, as he took command of the ragtag American Revolutionary forces in the very spot where this hotel is. It's not one of those "Washington Slept Here" kind of places. Because that's up the street at the Longfellow House. Which is nice, but they won't let you sleep there. I tried one night after a poetry reading, under the big willow tree. No go. But the Commander Hotel has cool bas-reliefs of George Washington in the lobby. They have a diorama of him surveying his men near the bathrooms. We poets always used to drink at the Commander Hotel bar because of me. I made everyone go there. I love hotel bars. No local people ever think of going there. And hotel bars usually have pool tables and cheap beer and you can meet strangers from distant places and beat them at pool.

The Commander Hotel has no pool tables, though, and it was almost entirely empty all the time. So we could roll in after a poetry reading and just own the place. Get the Red Sox on the TV. Order up a bunch of food. Getting loud with the poets. Arguing about whether Charles Olson could beat up Robert Creeley. That kind of thing. There's just something about this hotel that makes me want to grow old and live and die there, with all its wild George Washington stuff. I want more George Washington stuff. Every room should have a George Washington portrait, watching you with those cool portrait eyes that follow you around the room wherever you go. The bathroom especially. There should be a cherry tree in every room, with maybe a little plastic axe. So you can take selfies in a white-powdered wig with a wooden grin like you're gonna chop down that tree. It is wonderful to stay in hotels. It is terrible to ever have to check out.

Quit Whining and Be Up for Anything

You might not glean this from my writing, with which I am try-ing to cast myself in the most positive possible light and make myself sound as charming as I possibly can. But I can be a bit of a whiner. I do not want to do most things or go to most places or meet most people. People say, "Let's get a drink sometime." And I think, "Oh, sure, let's get a drink." And then as the day gets closer, I get filled with dread. What if I can't think of anything charming to say? What if I have no jokes? Why am I going out with this per-son? When I could be home, screwing around on the Internet in my underpants and watching *Seinfeld* episodes. Which I do practi-cally every night. Just hang out and watch *Seinfeld*s over and over again. The dread overcomes me. I start to panic. What if this person punches me? That's irrational; I haven't been punched in a while. But I really don't want to be! Anyway, I cancel. I stay home. I meet no one. I drink with very few people. I like meeting new people! Maybe they will be my soul mate, I think. But then, I don't know. They're probably not. I like doing things spontaneously. If you say, "Hey, let's right now go to the zoo." I'd be like, "Sure." And we'd go to the zoo. But if you say, "Hey, let's go to the zoo next week," I'll think, "Sure." And then, in the meantime, I will completely talk myself out of going to the zoo with you. Nothing personal.

So this makes me a rather reluctant traveler, when everything must be booked way in advance and such. I am traveling next week. To Maine. To hang out with my friends and fish and drink Moxie. I have visited this place many times. Do I know what day I will head up there? No. Will I take a car, train, or bus? I have no idea. Will I visit my parents on the way up or the way back? Beats me. I don't plan that far ahead. I like to have all kinds of options available to me. Perhaps I will meet a beautiful poet with a Porsche who will want to drive me all the way to central Maine. It could happen.

My brother had a wedding in the Florida Keys. Destination weddings could be worse than the Florida Keys. But I had just never even imagined going there. I dreaded going. I was too broke to afford the hotel, so I'd have to stay on the pullout couch in my parents' room. And weddings. I am happy for everyone who ever gets married. But just go elope. You know? I will buy a blender on eBay and send it to you. But then just stay married forever. I don't want to hear about your married problems, how hard it is to be married, how marriage is different than you ever expected. Beats me. I never got married. I am hideous and unlovable and no one will ever marry me. Do I whine about it? Sometimes. But not as much as married people whine about something.

So my brother was getting married in the Florida Keys. You gotta go, you gotta go. OK. So I'm sleeping on the pullout couch. Feeling like the victim of the universe, hideously alone with no one to joke about it with the entire time. So just me alone with my thoughts, which are generally horrible, for an entire weekend. Pretty rough. So the day of the wedding comes and I am kinda wandering around. And my father says, "Let's take a drive." And I say, "OK." Usually when my dad wants me to do something, it's, like, take out the trash. Or stop talking during the Patriots game. But, OK, sure. And we get into his car.

I am a delightful passenger. I take it all in, make jokes, play with the radio. I'm a terrible actual driver. But as far as passengers go, I'm fun to have around. My father is maybe the only one who doesn't appreciate my humor, or at least doesn't bother to humor my humor. But I respect him and look up to him. He was an IRS agent for, like, forty years, working hard in Boston, taxing people. But for all the time we spent together in the same town, commuting together, we maybe had lunch together only a handful of times. He did his thing and I did mine. I think fondly of the times we had lunch, but I went to Boston to try to be a different person than I had been in the lazy northern suburbs. And my dad went there to be a G-man. He came home tired; I moved out and stayed in Boston. I wouldn't say I have a complicated relationship with my father. He is a dad and I am a son. And we love each other, but that doesn't mean we hang out all the time. So I went into this car trip with some sort of trepidation. Would my father ask me what the hell I was doing with my life? Was there an agenda? Would he try to console me for my little brother getting married before me?

It turns out no. My father just thought that he'd probably never be on this part of the planet ever again. And, so, why not drive from the top of the keys to Key West and back? Sounded OK to me.

I would probably never be in this part of the world again, either. Unless my brother had some sort of fiftieth-anniversary party down the road that we all had to come to someday. We drove. The road is incredibly narrow. Usually just two lanes, and then just some beach on both sides. You can watch amazing sunrises or sunsets simply by crossing the street at the right time. The water is ridiculously clean-looking and blue. And the weather was always wonderful. Clouds drifted by, blocked the sun for a second. We talked the whole way about nothing specific. Just riding the curves from one key to the next. There'd be a sign: KEY BOYSENBERRY. OK, we're on another key. And then another sign: KEY FRUCTOSE. OK. Just kind of curving along at a cruise, winding our way off the American continent. I thought I hated islands! But peninsulas are way more nerve-racking. Just a big wave could practically wash everything away! Give me land, lots of land! But what bad could possibly happen to me? I'm with my dad. We're just making our way down to Key West at a leisurely pace. What time is that wedding anyway? Shouldn't we be getting ready? I imagine people will be wondering where we are. Worried prewedding people. Will we get in trouble? I don't know. My dad is here. Is it possible for him to ever get in trouble? He is the one who we usually get in trouble with!

But for a while all the whining I'd done (or would do) floated away like a puff. It was a beautiful day. We were making our way. Would traffic be bad on the way back? Would we miss the wedding and forever be outcasts? No. It was just me and my dad in a car, when we probably should have been somewhere else doing something else. Tying ties. Nothing really happened on this trip to Key West and back to the wedding, but it was one of the most satisfying trips I've ever taken. All because he said get in the car and I said OK.

No Headphones!

I went for a long time without wearing them or listening to music in the city, because I felt like if I did, I'd miss out on something essential. The sounds of New York. I thought I'd learn something important about myself and this place where I have decided to live, even if it is so expensive. I thought I'd appreciate the clamor. But most of what living in New York is all about as you walk around is overhearing terrible conversations, or people asking you for money, or just people being crazy. At least 75 percent of your waking day is spent overhearing stuff you'd rather not, or people making you feel bad enough to give them a buck. And so headphones are essential. But there is something to not wearing them while you're on the road. Or not wearing them all the time. Or not having to wear them all the time. Or something.

Yes, the soundtrack to your everything could be whatever is always happening on your iPod anyway. I have tended to make mixtapes for road trips; that's usually fun, and if ever we lose all technology and go back to mixtapes, I will be the first one in line. Road music is essential for all long trips. It's just those headphones. Why not share your traveling music with whoever you pick up along the way? When you're on the highway with all your friends, you do not all wear headphones and listen to whatever you have on your iPods. Or maybe we do now. I don't know. I go to parties and everyone is on their phones. I don't know if that means that I hate parties or I hate phones. Or if I just hate phones at parties. Everybody put your phone in a fishbowl and hang out at the party for a while!

And people are gonna talk to you whether you're wearing headphones or not. Most people are louder than my damned headphones. Which I usually step on eventually. As much as I like to drown out my own endless, reeling thought process with the same bunch of songs over and over (right now Bob Dylan breakup records, but sometimes Louvin Brothers gospel music), it is nice sometimes to overhear something. Especially when you're in a new place. And they use words like "yins" or "Grosse Gutt" or something. Or have awesome accents. Or weird bird sounds. From Saint Louis, the only thing I remember vividly is the frozen custard and the sound of cicadas. I know this year was supposed to be the year of the cicada, but that show never came to North Jersey or the Upper West Side, I guess. They were loud, the air was mayo-thick, and I will never forget the sound. Soon our headphones will be inside our heads. I was talking about this with my friend Sean, who works on the radio. I said, "What is the future of radio?"

And he said, "I don't know." And I told him they should put radios inside people's heads so that people could listen to stuff and no one else would know. They'd be listening to Kool Moe Dee while you're talking to them about some Excel spreadsheet. He said that was a great idea. So, that's happening. And you will like it.

But until then, maybe take them off once in a while. I think we need to experience things somehow that we neither want nor expect to, but that will become valuable to us down the road. The only cell phone conversation I ever wished I'd overheard was one with somebody barking: "Don't cut the black wire! Gently tug at the red wire! And then gently snip it away in one piece. No! Not the black wire! The red wire! If you cut the black wire, we'll miss you at Thanksgiving!"

I rode around the country on planes, buses, boats. I hate planes now. I used to like planes and sitting next to the window and looking out. But now, no. I sit on the aisle. I try to pretend I'm not on a plane. Like maybe I'm just inside a plane-themed restaurant. This is what I try to convince myself. I'm not afraid of dying, but I am afraid of dying on a plane. And I listen every time they do that big long speech about what floats and who should get the oxygen first. I listen every time, then immediately forget and am convinced that if something goes wrong, I will be eaten first. This is why I don't wear headphones on planes! Maybe everyone is talking about how you are the one who will be eaten first. You definitely want to overhear that discussion and pipe in, before it gets too out of control. Just to nip it in the bud, this loose talk of cannibalism. I might have headphones on, but that's just because I want you to talk about me. I am trying to lure you into a comfortable casual conversation that you think I won't overhear, so I can overhear it. And then I will know your plan for me, especially if it involves eating me first when the plane goes down.

When I actually do wear headphones on planes, specifically JetBlue planes, the ones with TVs and all the channels, I usually have no idea who's sitting next to me. They'll get up and go to the bathroom and come back and I'll be like, "Who is this person? Why do they want me to stand up?" Headphones bring us one step closer to becoming VCRs, with the 12:00 always flashing in our eyes. There is nothing like an actual good encounter with a stranger we just never thought we'd have. I revel in thirty-second relationships. In some ways I am at my best when I know I will never encounter you again. Like you, reader, finishing this up. I did not get to tell you everything about traveling. I surely did not tell you how to do it. In some ways I probably told you to not do it with me. And it definitely took you more than thirty seconds to read this whole thing. Which is terribly late getting to where it needs to go. I sat and planned it and agonized over it. Writing is like traveling, you make all these plans and try to think of everything, and then you forget everything and as you go a million other things come to you. Maybe we're just more aware of the possibilities of everything when we're traveling or writing. Maybe we're just open to a few more new experiences. It did seem to make sense to take this journey with you, across the pages, to and from all my past travels. That did seem to be something allegedly worth doing. Thanks. We all definitely survived it. We all definitely got from here to there. Unless you choked on one of those sandwiches with the fries in the middle. And you're facedown on your Kindle right now. In that case, thanks for spending your last few minutes in my company.

MADAME'S CANE

Anne Helen Petersen

You've heard this story before. Clarification: you've heard this story before if you reside within the not altogether rarefied demographic of middle- to upper-class students who studied abroad at some point in their college or postcollege career. Sometimes the details are slightly different—one of my friends went to Vietnam; another spent at least a month in the backwoods of Ecuador making pottery with an eighty-year-old master.

But the reason so many people undertake the voyage that so many others in their place have before—that's not too difficult to understand. Studying abroad in Europe isn't a pilgrimage, nor does it aim to reenact some nostalgic understanding of what our parents and grandparents did when they were our age. When my grandparents were our age, they were fighting in *the war*—or at least hanging out with "ladies of the night" in France, which I learned only when I had been ensconced in France and reading the cat scratch of my rapidly fading paternal grandfather, who slipped a note into the otherwise very chaste letter from my grandmother.

Studying abroad isn't necessarily a "thing" to which Generation X lays claim. But I did it right on the cusp—I mean, I was that thirteen-year-old watching *Reality Bites* and wishing that generation was mine; that student reading *Generation X* in the first semester of college and analyzing it instead of living it.

But my generation of study-abroaders, we were no millennials. My first year of college marked the first year of all-campus Ethernet. No one had a cell phone. When we wanted to find someone on campus, we walked a-fucking-round. Laptops were rare; AIM reigned supreme. But I don't mean to be nostalgic for transitory digital culture so much as set the stage for what it meant to go abroad at the beginning of 2002: airline tickets were ridiculously cheap (Seattle to Paris: $450); everyone kept telling you to sew Canadian flag patches to your backpack; and the guiding understanding of communication was that you'd write letters and send a few emails and maybe call if you figured out the complicated "SIM card system" that seemed to characterize all European cell phone economies.

Let it be said that I was completely okay with this scenario. I have hated talking on the phone since I was a small child and ran away from the receiver even when it was a plump Norwegian relative who simply wanted to talk about my new American Girl doll. When I was in junior high, I loved "note culture" because it meant that I didn't have to say anything aloud; I could convey it all in a well-crafted note that I may or may not have spent more time elaborately folding than actually writing.

I was one of those kids who spent all summer at camps (Science, Math, French, Overarching Nerd), where I accumulated pen pals like neuroses. There was nothing I loved more than sitting down and crafting a five-page letter, written in my exquisite and very unique left-handed penmanship, and making sure that the sender thought I was very, very sophisticated and very, very romantic: Did I meet you in an AOL chat room and you're from Ohio and all I know is that we feel the same way about the lyrics to Smashing Pumpkins' "Disarm"? Great. Give me your address.

By the time I reached college, that impulse had only slightly tempered. I spent an entire summer as a counselor at a camp where I had access to the Internet once a month and didn't even care. My best girlfriends from school wrote me elaborate letters with lots of markers and stickers, straight-up third-grade style. I was never hungover, ate a lot of trail mix, got a sweet one-piece tan, and won the Mail Contest every day. It wasn't a bad life.

And then friends started studying abroad. The first semester that this happens—especially at a small liberal arts college where you know everyone and feel as if the presence of all 1,200 students is intricately knit into your social well-being—you feel adrift. I felt especially adrift given that the boy that I loved, you know, that boy, the one who tortures you all four years of college and four years after—that boy had gone to a country so exotic and specific that I can't even name it. I was dating someone else but That Boy wrote me on homemade paper with a return address in a script so intoxicatingly foreign. I was a goner. I wanted to go away and write those letters at all times.

So I went to France. Not Paris, though—I knew that Paris was for:

a) People with serious aspirations about living on the Left Bank and becoming *artistes* and going Full Beret; or

b) Suckers. Namely, suckers who get stuck in a crappy homestay with someone who rents out rooms to make rent, rather than to have inculcating discussions with a very learned college junior from the sticks.

Plus, I'd already been to Paris before. Like a zillion times, like all the other privileged Idaho dorks in seventh grade whose parents took them to France and who then spent most of the time scowling at the camera while wearing very purposeful outfits of Umbro shorts, high socks, and Adidas T-shirts. Plus, after I'd exhausted the resources of French Immersion Camp, the last step was a full month in France—a week in Paris, two weeks in Saint-Malo, a final week with a host family. My mortification (I killed a French chicken with my own hands and went to a French party where I declined wine) and French training were effectively complete.

I was ready, in other words, for a real French town.

Nantes fit the bill. Two and a half hours from Paris by TGV, it was the French capital of the triangular slave trade, a past now far closeted and manifest only in the beautiful architecture by the *quais*. Jules Verne grew up there; the Edict of Nantes, signed by Henri IV, obviously went down there. It's a classic, midsize European city—everyone in France knows of it; few outside of France do. Residents speak English but refuse to, the way good French people should. The seafood is effervescently fresh. The Loire and Erdre Rivers meet there. It's sister city is Seattle, which should make some climate realities clear.

The weeks leading up to any study abroad are a mix of boredom, overplanning, and very careful outfit selection. Or maybe that's just for type A pre-abroaders like me, because chances are many of you were out getting wasted the night before and stuffed a ton of shit into a giant suitcase at 3:00 a.m. Either way, I got to Nantes, and in short order disposed of my carefully chosen wardrobe in favor of clothing purchased at the French *soldes*, which, confusingly enough, is actually the word for "massive sales at the end of each clothing season." I had a few weeks with my J.Crew polo shirts and Banana Republic jeans; then it was all tight black pants, H&M poly sweaters, and heeled black boots. As soon as I made my way to London, I bought a full-length black wool coat at a market in Piccadilly

Circus. I was ready to blend in with some Europeans like a totally self-conscious boss.

Even with the help of *les soldes*, it took some time. My French was great but not awesome. I wrote notes to my French mother, Madame Nadeau, and she very kindly added all the extra *e*'s I was leaving off basically everything. I insisted on going running, which, at least in France in 2002, was like insisting on margarine instead of butter at dinner: totally fucking unacceptable. The men I did see running were swarthy, sweaty simulacrums of '80s jogging commercials, complete with short-shorts. The women ran in T-shirts and ordinary bras. The breast dexterity was astonishing. This was before Lululemon and streamlined, overpriced workout gear, but still, the very existence of a sports bra made me look like a professional athlete, which is to say totally and utterly un-French.

Life fell into place. My classes, conducted totally in French, were preposterously easy. After two and a half years spent a) studying, b) drinking, c) fashioning theme costumes to go drink in, with major emphasis on a), I didn't know what to do with myself. One hour of homework a night? No homework on weekends? The only thing that took time was handwriting my essays on that exquisite, multilined French notebook paper.

Not since I slogged through criminally unchallenging high school in a small northern Idaho town had I had so much time on my hands. There was a two-euro movie theater five blocks from my school, so I started going to a movie nearly every day. They had American retrospectives, six-month-old French releases, and, most important, at least fifteen different films showing every day, starting at 10:00 a.m. and ending past midnight. I started by watching only films in English with French subtitles; by the end of the year I was watching *Mulholland Drive* totally in French, *sans sous-titres*, thus compounding the freak-out factor by ten. I screened the entire Scorsese oeuvre. I consumed crazy art films I'd only read about in world cinema texts. (Note to the wise: do not watch *The Piano Teacher* during your first four weeks abroad.) I watched *Amélie* five times. They let you bring in large tote bags and eat anything you want, and one of my best, hazy memories is drinking (most of) a bottle of red wine at 3:00 p.m. while watching *Moulin Rouge* in horribly dubbed French. It was perfect.

I also started walking everywhere. But not just like a French person—like a crazy person. I lived three miles from school. All the normal people—normal French people included—took the bus from where I lived to the central area of town. But I walked that shit; I walked that shit proud. I'd start my walk at the morning magic hour and watch the sun rising over the river. In France, looking someone in the eye as you pass is still considered a come-on, and I refined my ability to look straight through all the well-dressed, well-scarfed men who crossed my path.

I loved gauging my progress by the number of Catholic churches I'd pass: five, plus one giant, hideous afterthought of a Middle Ages cathedral. According to Madame Nadeau, one of the churches was home to a group of cloistered nuns who emerged from the walls just once a year to vote. Every day, I'd peer over the walls, hoping for a chance sighting, which happened only once: out of the corner of my eye, a glimpse of two nuns, hand in hand, disappearing around the garden wall. It was my secret to keep.

I learned how to cross streets like a European, which is to say I learned how to jaywalk, almost get run over, and stare cars in the eyes until they stopped for me. It was as if I was gaining gumption by the day, only I had no one to use it on—the roundness of my face, the pure Scandinavian-ness of it, compounded by my unfashionable haircut, gave me away as non-French. My only boyfriends were the bakers at the *boulangerie* where I fetched Madame's baguette on the way home from school, but they all had white hair and bellies straight out of a Disney cartoon.

The boy I had been dating was across the world, abroad in his own foreign time zone, but experiencing the inverse of my own experience. He was speaking English, going in with a bunch of other kids to buy a jalopy of a used car and drive it into the ground as they adventured through caves and cascading waterfalls and mountain peaks. And there I was, wearing tight black pants and practicing not looking people in the eye.

Still, he wrote me every day. Every day, a new letter, postcard, or package arrived. He wrote in a journal and then tore the pages out; by the end of the term, the entire journal had made its way to me. We weren't together, but we were aching for each other in the way that you do when you're in a foreign place for more than two weeks and beset by a unique and penetrating form of loneliness. I'd fall asleep every night with my Discman, listening to the CD he'd made for me. Highlights: an acoustic version of David Gray's "Please Forgive Me"; Elliot Smith's "Between the Bars." *Sad Sack Mix 2002* indeed.

It's a strange thing, that limbo between in and out of love at age twenty. I wanted to love him, I knew I didn't, I needed to love him, I knew I couldn't. Whether he knew the same was unclear. I'm certain I hurt him very deeply, all the comings and goings, promises and retreats. But the new rhythms and old insecurities of being abroad undercut the best of moral intentions.

But while I was busy slowly breaking and mending the heart of my ex-boyfriend, I was also figuring out how to travel. I'd accumulated two close friends via my program: one, Rebecca, was from my own college; the other, Kenna, told people that she "went to school in

Jersey" to avoid having discussions about going to Princeton. We were a gruesome threesome: three type A girls, non-complainers, exhaustive in our pursuit of local culture, opportunities to binge drink, and museums in which to be slightly hungover.

Over five months, we traveled all over Western Europe, treading the Eastern European line. At first, we were methodical: a very well-planned trip through Belgium, Munich, and Prague. We had hostels picked out ahead of time. We reserved a sleeper car. We froze our faces off on the Charles Bridge in Prague and visited all of the appropriate heritage sites.

Overplanning had its benefits: there was much less of the "I just got off the train and I'm starving and don't you dare make me look at another hostel let's just eat bread in this park fuck this." But it also meant that the only hostel we could book online was, unbeknownst to us, in the mid-suburbs, a solid subway ride and transfer from the center of town. Instead of guitar-playing, slightly smelly bohemian Americans, this hostel was filled with very polite and clean Czech twentysomethings in town for much more pragmatic reasons than to get drunk on Pilsner Urquell for pennies.

We blended in horribly. Kenna and I ran every morning and every morning we got lost, each time more intricately than the last. We were deep enough into the city that the evidence of Soviet rule was still very much in evidence: concrete, giant statues, more concrete. But beneath, signs of life before Communism: in a dilapidated, overgrown park, the remains of a beautiful fresco pathway, buried in years of graffiti and rotting foliage. At one point we thought we'd found a shortcut; turns out it was just a labyrinth surrounded by barbed wire, which we tried to sneak under but instead ended up cutting our running shirts to shred on the barbs. We regularly ran double what we'd intended, returning to the room bloodied, a nest of twigs in Kenna's curly hair.

One night, we decided to go to dinner around the corner, in a place with little signage yet always filled with people. Inside, there were no small tables, just long tables for six to ten. The waitress took us and our wide eyes over to one of the tables, where three grandpa-aged men had sprawled out a sea of beer glasses and animal carcasses. She said some choice words to the grandpas in Czech, and suddenly the sea was migrating to one end of the table. She handed us menus, ignored our looks of helplessness, and retreated.

In tourist areas in most countries, even in countries where few are fluent in English, menus are paired with vivid, overexposed photos of the dishes. You look; you guess at the animal or vegetable depicted; you choose. Not here. We had a rumpled page of handwritten Czech, with all the terrifying accent marks in all the unexpected places. After puzzling for a bit, the grandpas, who'd been looking at us in a non-ogling way for the past five minutes, called the waitress over, gestured toward us, and begin speaking. They held up some fingers, made a gesture of guzzling a giant beer, which we interpreted as the universal sign for "Yes, you like to drink grandpa beer?"

The waitress nodded and left, returning with three overflowing mugs of pilsner. Fifteen minutes later, she returned again: more beer, plus three massive plates of what looked to be three complete animals. A tremendous white-fleshed fish, a rabbit (sans head and fur), a fowl of some sort (minus head, feet, feathers). All had been roasted in something delicious and paired with a goulash of indeterminate vegetables, all perfect.

We demolished those plates. More beers came, which we downed like water, like something that actually aids the process of digestion. The Czech grandpas were so jolly and pleased and kept asking us whether we were enjoying it in their best pantomime. We so very clearly were. The bill was somewhere around $5. We rolled home, filled with benevolence sliding toward sleep.

Traveling by train is an exercise in precision food-wise. Unless you want to get stuck with warm beers from a vending machine (something I very much did, once, to a very bad end) as your only nourishment, you have to pack yourself a meal. The French do this so well, and with such care, that everything we did looked like the work of clumsy, ravenous five-year-olds. Our baguettes were stuffed in our backpacks; the French had theirs carefully wrapped in adorable checkered cloths, apparently made precisely for the occasion. Our market-purchased carrots still had dirt on them; the French had theirs steamed with a sprinkling of parsley. When we ran out of food, we ate LU cookies, which you'd recognize if you saw—usually they cost about ten dollars a box at import stores—offered to us by our French families. Principal ingredients: butter and butter. Our crumbs got everywhere. Seatmates looked at us with pity bordering on disgust. Or possibly the opposite.

And then there was the matter of the tuna. Even today, I smell tuna and I think of cross-European train rides. I dislike tuna, but you know who likes tuna? My cheap-ass traveling companions. They hauled stashes of canned tuna across Europe, draining the liquid in the bathrooms. People bitch about Americans being rude, being drunk, being disrespectful in public spaces, but usually they are not talking about draining canned tuna in train bathrooms. But perhaps they should be. That shit was *flagrant*.

We ate giant pretzels in Munich and marveled at the sight of mannequins whose measurements, unlike the *petite* French ones, approximated our own. A friend of a friend picked us up in Belgium, took us to a club filled with house music, arranged bottle service, and then took us to his parents' house (?!?) so that we could each take long, luxurious showers and wash off the travel stink. He then proceeded to try to make out with each one of us. We left very early the next morning, hopped a train to Bruges, and walked around in the rain, drinking tea in four different establishments simply to keep warm until a hostel let us in.

When we went to London to visit my best friend, we naturally took several bottles of wine with us. On the Chunnel, without a corkscrew. But we were pros, using the end of a borrowed fork to push the cork down into the wine. Just be careful of the first pour, because the way that gravity/physics/life works will ensure that you splatter red wine all over your person if you're not careful. We thought the trip was two hours, but an unanticipated time change made it more like three and a half. Point being: all wine had been drunk by the time we reached London. Which also meant that we were drunk enough to completely miss my best friend, who had come to fetch us, as she had been thoroughly Londonized in just over two months: dark eyeliner, cropped red-leather jacket, heels that seemingly extended to her hips. This was a girl who had regularly sported clogs and tank tops as "dress up" gear back on campus: no wonder we'd passed her by.

This was also a girl with whom I had spent my entire college life. Along with a cluster of four other girls, we had essentially grown and regressed and traded clothes and proofread papers and gotten drunk together for the past two and a half years, with very brief breaks for summer. Now, we were still doing all those things, but we were doing them individually—and thus in separate directions. The friend in Spain, a lifelong vegetarian, was constantly hungry; the friend in Australia was incessantly hazed, constantly overheated, and disillusioned. We were growing and regressing, as always, but without one another, save the weekly group email and, for those of us in Europe, the occasional discombobulating visit. When we all returned, it would take a solid month to reroot ourselves in one another, in common experience and understanding. Our distance from one another was healthy, was certainly productive—but I missed them more than anything else American.

Back in the customs line off the Chunnel, we still had wine in our backpacks, ostensibly to gift to our new London friends, and it weighed us down so much that by the time we made it to the front of the line, we tipped over like classic American assholes. It would all have been very embarrassing had I been sober enough to realize as much.

London was a haze of Strongbow and our own versions of dark eyeliner—plus Indian food and "club wear" purchased at H&M. It all felt very out of body, and not just because I was essentially hungover the entire time. Suddenly we were surrounded by people speaking our language—there was even a Starbucks nearby. But we were still wearing the wrong clothes; even English felt wrong in our mouths. I felt alienated from my own alienation. I needed to get back to Nantes as soon as possible, where I could feel out of place in a way that had become comfortably familiar.

There's something about studying abroad, and about college generally, that facilitates weird eating habits. Eating disorders, sure, but also the JV brand of eating disorders, which I once heard someone call "disordered eating," or, by its more common description, "drinking a lot of Diet Coke and making meals of popcorn." With my Norwegian frame, all extra weight on my body accumulates where Norwegians need it most: right in the belly, where it can keep your vital organs most warm.

In the age of the Britney stomach, this just wasn't okay. I was never overweight, but I was a self-conscious girl who was even more self-conscious about her stomach, and the stories I'd heard, seemingly from everywhere concerning the "freshman fifteen" did nothing to help my confidence. My greatest fear as a freshman at a prestigious liberal arts college wasn't about getting a B. It was about gaining weight and people talking about me.

By the time I went abroad, I had a strategy down: eat things that ostensibly have a low calorie count (raisin bran for lunch); exercise a ton; eat things when drunk that sober self would never eat. Ultimately, it balanced out, but it was certainly never healthy. Now I know that I was doing something called "exercise anorexia," in which you work very hard to burn off more calories than you consume, but at the time I just thought I was spending a lot of time on the elliptical, doing lots of step aerobics (Holla, 2000!) and getting all my necessary nutrients from a dinner that mostly consisted of leafy greens and soft-serve frozen yogurt, to be followed by a 1:00 a.m. snack of frat house nachos and Busch Light.

Like most disordered eating, it arose from a lack of control. In the dorms, I couldn't make my own food; therefore, I tried to control what I could eat and what calories I'd consume. When you move abroad, your food is once again regimented, only this time it's shaded with the peculiar shame of trying to appease/not offend your host family. Butter on everything? Sure! Bread at every meal? Fabulous!

I realize that "French people don't get fat" and all that nonsense, but people studying abroad *do* get fat and the culprit is (a) pastries, (b) two-euro bottles of wine, (c) more pastries, and (d) the chocolate muesli they sell at French supermarkets that's like hippie crack.

If I ate everything that my French grandmother made me, walked all the time, drank like a responsible adult, and avoided the muesli, chances are high I would've returned looking exactly the way I did when I left. But I was scared. Of many things, clearly, but also of the same fate that supposedly befalls freshman girls. And the lack of homework only made obsessive exercising easier: I even joined a French gym, filled with French women clad in approximations of '80s American workout gear, where I took classes in *abdos-fessiers* ("abs-butts") complete with very graphic air-humping sessions. In the gym, which smelled of old socks, you could find five different "vibrating" stations featuring large bands of fabric that you'd place across your "problem areas"; you'd turn the machine on and let it do its magic. This was not 24-Hour Fitness.

It was mostly worthless, fitness-wise, but it was a place to stop on the way home—a point of conversation, something to write home about. Your friends and family want only so many descriptions of the five-course meals prepared for you every night—they also want the dorky French people, the stories about the esteemed garden in the center of the town that kept stubby-antlered deer tethered in the corner. The unexpected, the abject, the things that made France and what you were doing more weird, and thus less desirable, than America and what they were doing.

When we were traveling outside of Nantes, I tried to run and did a lot of crazy walking, but mostly we adopted the following strategy:

- Breakfast—coffee
- Lunch—a piece of fruit; Diet Coke
- Dinner—drinks purchased from street vendor and consumed on the street (especially true in Italy and Greece); giant dinner; local dessert.

It's classic yo-yo dieting, only we did it over the span of a day, every day. It became our normal. When friends met up with us while traveling, they scoffed at our refusal to stop for lunch. But we were the normal ones; they were the weird ones insisting on actual nutrition.

You adopt all sorts of weird habits while traveling: the order of operations when you first get on the train; how long you'll wait before getting really desperate for a bathroom; how many hostels you visit before deciding which one was the perfect balance between cheap and bedbugs. I used to listen to the same four songs every night because it was the only thing that kept me steady when my life seemed so rudderless.

In truth, my life was fairly set. In four months, I'd return home, have a lush internship, spend most of the time getting tan, and start my senior year. But that aimless hour between 4:00 and 5:00 p.m., when you've visited all the museums and cultural centers and browsed the postcards and should be hungry but aren't, because you've taught your body not to feel it, and it's too early to drink but too close to dinner to go back to your room—that's when you feel empty and aimless.

There was a feeling that I'd get when walking home in Nantes— when the light was slanting over the cathedral and catching the invisible dust in the air, when you could feel the exhilaration and exhaustion of everyone going home from work, when the kabob shops were just opening for business, when the café patrons started overflowing onto the streets, with their small, squat glasses of red wine and long-stemmed glasses of kir. I loved walking through it, with my high heels and my newly leveled gaze, but I also felt very much excluded.

French teens and young adults are not the type to include foreigners. Some call this snobbery, but I just understood it as tradition. Madame Nadeau frankly explained it to me: The French make friends early—like childhood early—and then they stick with those friends, usually for life. They go to high school with those friends and they go to college with those friends—in France, as in most

European countries, college is free and public, with little significant difference between universities. The drift and displacement—the quilt work of friendship that many Americans accumulate over the course of high school, college, and grad school—was as foreign to most French as the taste of *boeuf tartare* was to me. With such close-knit friend groups, there was little incentive to welcome outsiders, particularly outsiders who spoke the language at the level of a twelve-year-old.

It was, in other words, hard to make friends. Indeed, my best friend was Madame Nadeau. She was what the French call *une madame d'une certaine âge,* which simply meant that she was somewhere between fifty and seventy years old and worthy of your respect. I loved the weird, retired rhythms of her day—the way she'd wake up, turn on the radio in her bedroom, and just lie in bed for an hour, taking in the day and its promises. She was of the generation of French women that would bathe once, maybe twice, a week yet always look perfectly "finished," as my copies of 1920s fan magazines put it. She had two colors of bold lipstick and salt-and-pepper hair she'd sweep up into an elegant chignon. Like most French women, she had a way with scarves that I will never be able to approximate. She spent her days making flowers grow on her porch and making the tour of various food providers: the *poissonnerie*, her favorite vegetable stand, the *boucher*, the *fromagerie*.

She spoke no English save "Good appetite," the literal translation of *"Bon appétit."* She'd cook leeks with balsamic glaze and serve them whole; *coquilles Saint Jacques* (scallops) in the perfect amount of butter and white wine, paired with delicately braised white asparagus. She taught me how to flip *galettes*, but mostly she kept me out of the cooking space, placing me at the small breakfast table and plying me with a glass of wine that she knew, from much practice, would make it easier for me to speak French with her.

In the program, Madame Nadeau was known as one of the few host mothers who'd accept gay students. Ever since her husband, a physician, had passed away fifteen years earlier, she'd taken in students—mostly, as she told me, so she could justify cooking full five-course meals. Her first boarder was a refugee of sorts: a gay student who, through his frankness about his sexuality, had offended the sensibilities of the host couple. The director of the program asked her if she would house *un homosexual.* Her response: *"Pourquoi pas?"*

And so she'd hosted a steady stream of these men, whom she called *"juste un peu particulier"* and *"très amusant."* I was her first female student in nearly a decade, and I relished the mornings when she would tell me I looked *"très, très belle"* on the way out the door. She rarely volunteered information about herself but would answer all questions, especially after the fourth course, when she'd set out a plate of cheeses and ripe fruit, which she'd peel, perfectly, with a penknife.

After a dinner about halfway into my stay, we meandered toward the subject of The War. She'd been a young girl. Her family had been a member of the landed gentry, or the French approximation thereof, living in a modest château that had been in the family for centuries. The Germans had occupied Vichy France, forcing her family to live in an outbuilding while her parents maintained the farm and silently served the occupying forces. Madame's face, as she told the story, was one of old and well-worn disgust, but her knife remained steady on the apple in front of her.

One night, she recalled, the German soldiers had become uproariously drunk on wine from the cellar of the château. A candle tipped over; fire spread throughout the house, leaving the soldiers trapped on the second floor. Madame Naudeau's father was terrified: the house was a loss, but if the soldiers died, the blame for the deaths would be on the family. At the last minute, the dozen soldiers made the long leap to the ground—they broke bones, but they lived. As did Madame's family.

It was the type of story that sobers you and makes you feel completely drunk.

I don't know how we moved on to another topic. We said, *"Bon nuit"* and I retreated to my room, wrote some letters, but couldn't tell anyone what she'd just told me. Her own story evacuated all my own.

Every month Madame Nadeau went to *faire visite* with her old gentlemen and lady friends. They had a full dinner; they drank heavily on a weeknight because why wouldn't a pensioner; they played snipy games of bridge.

In April the game rotated to our apartment. I was invited to sit *à table* for drinks and dinner, which made me spectacularly nervous. But they made me a kir, complimented my accent, which they claimed was quickly becoming *"très Nantais, c'est parfait,"* and told stories of old Nantes, of how poorly Madame Nadeau played bridge (*bbbbbbbah, c'est faux!*). I was gossiping with seventy-year-olds. My glass was magically refilling. It was the least lonely, the most competent, I'd felt since arriving.

Still, I ran. I ran to have something to go home to; I ran to have something to do when I woke up. I ran to get to my friend's house, five miles away, and I ran to return. I ran along the river walk, where I could see all the French families out promenading their exquisitely dressed babies. I ran because it was a way to stop writing and reading and obsessing over letters.

It's not surprising that I ran until I hurt myself. I'd accumulated blisters, which, on the advice of my military ex-boyfriend, I covered with duct tape. It simultaneously was and was not a solution: yes, I didn't aggravate the blisters; no, I couldn't take the duct tape off. At some point, blisters grew on blisters, sloughed off, did something unspeakable until I had what amounted to a small hole in the arch of my foot, which promptly grew infected.

I went to the pharmacy, where my claim that "I have a small hole in my foot" was met with double the usual French dubiousness. I acquired some form of antibiotic ointment and should've stopped running. But my compulsion was too great.

Here's where I could tell you that my foot went gangrenous or I got trench foot or broke five bones. Nothing quite so dramatic. I simply favored it, thus straining a muscle in my left hip, but kept running, exacerbating a tweak into a tear.

All this a week before heading to the French Riviera with my program, where we'd walk for miles. I saw Cannes, I saw Monte Carlo, I saw Princess Grace's grave, I saw little dots before my eyes whenever I attempted to stand. By the end of the trip, I was in constant pain. As I hobbled my way through the aisle of the train, the head of my program—a true no-nonsense ballbuster with bright pink lipstick and a bangin' fifty-year-old body—told me what was what: she was taking me to the emergency room when we got off the train.

And so she did. She called Madame Nadeau. After they did a little collective *tssssk*ing, she zipped me downtown. It was the first time I'd been in a car since arriving in France, and she drove exactly the way I'd expect her to, briskly and without mercy.

The French emergency room was a marvel of socialism. It wasn't cleaner or better lit than an American emergency room; it was just easier. Everything was paid for—I was covered by my own insurance, my travel insurance, and the French government. A very young and incredibly handsome French doctor, assured that I was (near) fluent, asked me to take off my pants. The rest is a bit of a blur, perhaps induced by how embarrassing my underwear was, or perhaps it was the pain I experienced as he attempted to rotate my joints and locate the pain.

The doctor's orders were equally embarrassing: Stop moving so much. Take these Vicodin.

The problem, however, was my plane ticket to Athens, with a departure time in twenty hours. But the director of the program had a solution: we would borrow Madame Nadeau's backup cane (she used one, on and off, for her own bad hip), and I would successfully limp my way across the Aegean Sea without further exacerbating my injury.

Suddenly, there was I was, getting my cane through airport security. Stowing my cane in the overhead bin. Using my cane to walk through the Athens agora. Pointing my cane at skeezy dudes and making *PEW PEW PEW* sounds. We took the twelve-hour ferry to Santorini, the dramatic queen of the Greek islands, which I dozed through in a Vicodin-induced haze of near happiness.

The ferry reached Santorini at the magic hour and everything seemed primed for perfection. We started haggling with cab drivers until, suddenly, none remained. At the Santorini port, that's a legitimate problem: The island is in fact a caldera, a half-moon remnant of the massive volcano from tens of thousands of years ago. That remnant, however, is not flat—it is as if someone took a large knife and cut the volcano like a cake, leaving a sheer, steep cliffside on the section that remains.

There we were: three twenty-year-old girls, one cane, no cabs; at the bottom of the caldera, looking up at the lights slowly emerging from the whitewashed sugar cube houses perched on the cliffs above.

The bravest of us—the one we always made go talk to strangers, the one we made rent the moped and ask embarrassing questions and speak in foreign tongues—approached a pickup full of young Greek men who'd wandered in after the arrival of the ferry. She was beautiful in that feckless, coltish way—plus, she was Italian, which meant she looked Greek, with a mess of perfect curly hair and starling blue eyes, and which was why we got her to ask all the difficult questions.

And just like that, we were in the back of the pickup, cane tucked carefully beside me, wedged among sweaty travel-smelling bodies, hairpin-turning our way up the winding road. It was dangerous and ill conceived: everything they tell you not to do and everything you should, absolutely, do.

The sun had set twenty minutes before, and the sky was blue-blacking down. It was the warmest I'd felt in months. I hadn't emailed in weeks, hadn't spoken on the phone since January. All my sources of cathexis had been taken from me. I was still lonely, still half-empty, still hobbled.

But I had a cane.

THAT WITCH IS TIED UP

Edith Zimmerman

My friend Carrie and I were in an open-air market in Mexico City when an old man tried to lick her shoulder. She jumped, we turned around to look at him, and he held out a clear plastic bag filled with liquid. The liquid was brown and opaque, and we backed away but he followed, extending the bag toward us, and at some point we started nervously referring to it, in English and to each other, as a "bag of shit," although it was probably just a drink. I'm not even sure what he was doing to her shoulder; maybe it was all a lot more benign than we'd interpreted. But he kept following, holding out the bag, liquid sloshing, so we walked progressively faster, and so did he, until all three of us were basically running through the market. Eventually Carrie and I found an exit and crossed a street just as a stoplight turned colors, putting cars between us. *"Déjanos, pendejo!"* she yelled from our sidewalk—"Leave us alone, asshole!" Although it's rarely clear if you're the hero, the villain, or the idiot when traveling, and maybe you're always all three. Later on that same trip we snorkeled and I saw an eel swimming below us, or a sea snake, and I wasn't scared, despite the weeks I'd spent memorizing facts about snakes in the

guidebooks. One fact was that the sea snake is the most poison-
ous snake in the world, except that no one should worry, because
its jaw only opens wide enough to bite you on the webby flesh
between your thumb and index finger. I've told many people this
fact, although I don't even know if it's still true or ever was. I know
a similar "fact" about daddy longlegs.

A youngish bald man with almost spookily white-blue eyes checked
me in at the Blue Lagoon geothermal pool in Iceland. He spoke
perfect American English, and we struck up a conversation as he
gave me my towel and electronic wristband. It turned out his father
was from Cleveland and his mother was from Reykjavík (or the
other way around), and we exchanged email addresses to possibly
meet up later that week at a bar in town. It never happened, but I
wondered then and still wonder now how many people he'd been
giving (or still gives) his email address to. Anyway, I drifted through
the lagoon alone, drinking beer from a plastic cup, trying to figure
out where the clay everyone was smearing their faces with was. (In
wooden honey-pot-style boxes off to the sides, and on the lagoon
bottom.)

Another spa, in Stockholm, several years earlier. I was sixteen, with
my mom. It was a no-bathing-suits place, and she'd gone out first.
I took my time in the locker room, nervously undressing, preparing for the first time my mom would see me naked since I'd been a
kid. Because (as I reasoned), if I were her, I'd be curious to see how
I'd turned out—would my boobs look like hers? etc.—but also not
want to stare or freak me out. Anyway, I went into the spa, got into
a pool, and it was fine. Just a bunch of relaxed women hanging
around. If my mom noticed anything—and now I feel like I'm the
one making this weird—it never showed.

Las Vegas spa. No longer embarrassed by my own nakedness. We lay back with cucumbers over our eyes, but I hadn't actually known how to arrange them, so after a few minutes I took them off and examined my friend Carrie (another Carrie) lying serenely next to me. How do people learn these things? They go under the towel, aha. It was echoey and peaceful there, nearly empty, with pools and pools and pools. Our boobs floated in them, pre- and post-cucumber, and I remember acting slightly more at ease than I felt. Just having a normal conversation with my friend Carrie, but naked. So I guess I was a little embarrassed. Because we all want to stare at one another naked, right? Or: How do people graduate out of wanting to stare at one another naked? Should we?

Thanksgiving in London, with my mom, eating turkey sandwiches on our hotel bed, watching TV. I was in middle school, it was my first time out of the country, and in an attempt to seem cool (or to make my mom feel somehow like she'd imposed on me by taking me on this generous trip?), I never made an effort to adjust to the time difference, so I slept in the bathtub, where I stayed up most nights with the lights on reading *Lonesome Dove*.

My mom and I getting in a fight in the subway in Paris on the way to the airport, another trip. I was sixteen and carrying some of her luggage. She thought the airport was one way; I thought it was another—both required subway changes—and it got to the point where she said that if I really thought it was my way, I might as well go. Fine, I said, dumping her luggage at her feet. I walked off, and she didn't follow, so I got on the subway, changed trains, and went to the airport. I checked in, went to the gate, and felt a thrill when she wasn't there, which meant I'd won our stupid little standoff. But then the flight started boarding, and she still wasn't there. I didn't know what to do, so I just got on the plane, hoping she'd join me at the last minute. But she didn't, and then the plane took off, and then it landed in Boston. And she still wasn't anywhere when we got out—maybe she'd been hiding? I thought, but no—so I just took the subway home, and, unsurprisingly, she wasn't there, either. There weren't any messages on the machine, so I called the airline, and a representative told me Passenger [my mom] was on a flight to Chicago, which then connected to Boston, so I felt a little better and went to sleep. In the morning she was in the kitchen making coffee, and we didn't speak for a long time. Eventually she told me her purse had been grabbed in the subway, shortly after we'd parted ways, with her passport, wallet, and ticket inside. Weeks later the Parisian police would call to say they'd recovered her purse, minus her money and credit cards, although the only thing she wanted to know was whether the pair of earrings I'd made for her in grade school was still there—yellow Fimo suns with smiley faces.

The two-leg flight to Johannesburg was the longest I'd ever taken, and I must have not eaten enough, or eaten well enough, because by the time we began our landing, I was so hungry I'd become nauseated. There weren't any airsickness bags, so I threw up into the plastic wrapping that my lap blanket had come in. I was in the window seat, and the other people in my row had, until that point, been watching our descent. On that same trip, I saw the coolest animal I think I've ever seen in the wild, which was the kori bustard, a huge but generally blue jay–shaped bird, which made it unexpectedly hilarious and great. So, a giant brown blue jay. Like five feet tall. It had to run and flap its wings before it could fly, like a tiny plane taking off. It was amazing. It would be neat if more animals had that *Honey I Shrunk/Blew Up the Kids* vibe.

When I was twenty-five, I went home to Boston—Cambridge—to visit my family. A few nights in, I went out to a bar with a book, and I'd been reading for about half an hour, or a glass of wine long, maybe two, when the guy next to me asked what I was reading.

I didn't want to talk to anyone, but I held up the cover. "*2666*, by Roberto Bolaño," I said. "It's a three-part book," I added. I'm not sure why.

"Oh, I see," he said. "I was wondering about the 666."

I'd noticed this, too; because of the way the text wraps around the cover, to anyone on your right, it looks like you're reading a book called *666*. So I said, "It's about 2666, the year. I think. Not, like, the devil."

Then I made a show of looking back down at my book, but the guy kept asking questions, like what did I do, where did I live, etc., and it came out that I was only visiting—that I'd grown up there but now lived in New York. He told me he was from Ghana and doing a postgrad program at MIT. Eventually he asked me why I was visiting, and I guess I was feeling melodramatic, so I told him it was because my dad was dying, which was true.

"I'm sorry to hear that," he said. Then he told me he'd gotten a call a few weeks earlier that his own father had died, unexpectedly, at his family's home in Ghana, in the kitchen, of a heart attack. He also described the most recent time he'd visited his parents—three years ago—as well as the fight he and his dad had gotten into the last time they'd spoken, which was over the phone, months earlier. He told me the color of the telephone in his parents' kitchen—mint green—and how he pictured the way his father must have wrapped its cord around the table's legs as they'd argued. I told him about my situation, too. About the oversized stuffed bear a friend's young son had left in my dad's bedroom, and about how my dad had said it was fine to use his nickname instead of his full name if I ever had a kid and wanted to do that. A little while later, the guy and I said good night and parted ways.

Two days after, I went back to the same bar with a friend, and the guy was there again, and again alone, drinking a beer. I waved to him and he waved back. We didn't talk, and it made me a little sad that he was by himself, but he seemed perfectly happy. Besides, he'd said he liked the bar, and that he went there frequently.

A beautiful blonde Latvian girl at the Spanish language school in Málaga where I spent a summer warned me that the giant cockroach I'd bragged to her about killing had probably been filled with tiny babies, most of which she imagined were now finding new places to live in my room, or inside the shoe I'd squished it with. At another point she also told me that she never carried fewer than three pairs of sunglasses with her at all times so that she'd never have to squint in the sun and risk getting wrinkles, which is something that's stayed with me.

When I was seventeen, I went to Costa Rica to do community service with a teen group, although the whole thing was mostly so that we could look better on college applications. We'd spend the weekdays in a small town digging trenches and setting rebar for a soccer field that the town's residents were building, although I imagine we might have slowed things down as much as we sped them up. And then on weekends we'd go to various resort-type places, sneaking piña coladas and flirting with stoned expat surfers. In our small cabin during the week, though, we slept in tidy rows of sleeping bags on the floor with bug tents around our heads. (Bug tents are actually surprisingly soothing—sort of like little safety pyramids.) Anyway, the first night there, before any of the resort stuff, I woke up and realized that my hard little pillow was wet, but I couldn't figure out why. My ears were wet, too, but it was too dark to tell if they were bleeding, and because nothing hurt and I was too scared to get out of the bug tent and navigate my way to the outhouse, I just went back to sleep. In the morning everything had dried, although clumps of my hair were now somehow "inside" my ear. One of the group's leaders helped me figure out what must have happened, which was that the visor I'd brought to wear while trench digging had pushed my ears down and out, and the backs had gotten so sunburned that they'd blistered, opened, and then dried back up in the night, with my hair inside. She helped me wash them and pull the hair out, and then she made me little blue bandage-cuffs that looked like ear warmers.

The first thing I did in Reykjavík was go to a bar, where I struck up a conversation with the guy next to me, who introduced himself as one of Iceland's top ten rappers. One of the first things *he* did was make fun of his own tattoos—"cheesy" yin-yangs, sunbursts—and then he invited me to a "beer-drinking" party with him and his friends, or to smoke weed out back if I wanted, but I said no, although now I wish I'd done both. I also met a guy on the sidewalk at 4:00 a.m. one night while he was wearing a toilet seat around his neck. I'd thought we were both a little drunk, but it turned out he wasn't at all; in any case, we exchanged contact information, and a few days later he took me on an amazing tour of Reykjavík and the surrounding towns, including to a building he described as the president's home. We now follow each other on Instagram, and regularly like each other's photographs. I don't know, there's something I can't put my finger on that I like so much about this. Also nothing romantic happened and no overtures were made, although

I was probably hoping for it more than he was. Actually, I'm not entirely sure what was going on there.

In high school I got sick during a family cruise in Alaska—at the time I considered it whooping cough, but I think it was just a cold—and spent the majority of it in my room. The room had one porthole that looked out onto an interior passageway, and for a lot of the trip I'd just lain on the bed, fully clothed, staring out the porthole feeling sorry for myself. It was a small cruise—maybe forty passengers—and there was a small staff, too. One of them was this incredibly hot guy with golden-tan skin who always looked a little flustered, but in a sweet way, like he cared about what was going on and that it stressed him out. Anyway, one afternoon while I was lying in my bed, looking out the porthole, he passed by and for whatever reason turned to look in my direction. And for a moment we made eye contact. Prescription-grade benzoyl peroxide was dabbed in white mounds across my face because I had acne and couldn't think of anything to do in that room except cough, sleep, look in the mirror, and apply acne medication until it was time for a meal. We made eye contact another time when I was eating dinner with my family, but that was it.

One winter a few years ago, I traveled with a friend to visit his grandparents in Europe. The first night there I drank so much wine that the next day I threw up, and because the grandparents drank (modest amounts of) wine with both lunch and dinner, and invited us to do the same, and because I didn't have enough self-restraint, I kept drinking and never entirely recovered, and spent the rest of the trip about a quarter queasy. The food they prepared was out-standing, except (to me) for the one meal that consisted entirely (as far as I can remember) of lightly steamed sea snails distributed clatteringly into each of our bowls. There were ramekins of drawn butter to dip them into, and we each had a little fork to squelch-wrangle them out.

A friend and I were enjoying a traditional four-person live band at an Edinburgh pub one night—fiddles, guitar, chanties, etc.—so much that we bought a copy of the CD they were selling. Once we got back to America, my friend burned the CD to his computer and sent me the files. With an apology, because we hadn't noticed at the time, but one of the songs was about how if a man loves a woman enough, it's fine if he rapes her.

My dad, my stepmother, my two stepbrothers, and I were on a family trip to Switzerland. We were roughly in middle school, I think. Maybe Nat was in high school, I'm not sure, but we could buy alcohol legally there (or Nat could), because I remember we bought a six-pack of beer at a supermarket, and when we put it in Ben's backpack, it felt like we were in an alternate, futuristic universe. We smoked cigars, too—I guess we'd also bought them at the supermarket—and they were awful. Overwhelming and huge but also excellent, in their way. We were sitting on some terrace, just the three of us. Not even anywhere close to being adults, but feeling like we were. Maybe you always look back at moments when you feel adult and kind of shake your head. Perpetual head shaking.

For a change of pace during that weekend in Las Vegas, my friend Carrie and I went to the Atomic Testing Museum, which is a strange and wonderful place. Lots of rooms of varying fascination and boringness—and generally emptyish—and all of them filled with this subtle but overarching sense of dread, like, "Wait, *how* near are we to all this radioactivity? Is this bad? Have there been enough . . . years?" There was one display that had a Geiger counter, or something indicating that an area near us had recently been toxically radioactive, or something along those lines, and I remember backing away, as if being on the other side of the room would save me/us. Anyway, in the last of the exhibition rooms, there was one display showing what had happened to a test house after it had been exposed to an atomic bomb, in the '50s I think. They'd apparently set up a mannequin family in this model home, tested a bomb, and then—post-explosion—put the "mom" mannequin on display. She was lightly singed and missing a leg and an arm; her hair, dress, and face had all faded; and they'd tied her to an iron post with straw-colored rope. They'd also attached her arm to the wall beside her, which made it a sort of horrific and striking/baffling display, unless/until you read the description about why she was so mangled and de-limbed. While Carrie and I were reading it, a little boy and his father also came up to check her out. "Is that a witch?" the father asked his son, but the boy said nothing. "That witch is tied up!" the man said.

In Florence I climbed an ancient building up four-hundred-something stone steps, through progressively narrower and what felt like purposefully nightmarish spiral stairwells. And although the closeness was genuinely awful, I played up my "fear" so that it seemed like I hated the experience more because of this suddenly activated claustrophobia than because of how depressingly out of shape I was. I was with a guy. We weren't dating, but we also weren't NOT dating. Afterward we had lunch in a little gazebo-type restaurant nearby, and while I tried to pretend like I wasn't still catching my breath, he asked me how my drinking problem was going and what I planned to do about it. It was almost the end of our trip, which had been nice, although that issue had been sort of hanging over it. I was like, "I don't know, I don't know," and looked away and wanted to but didn't order another glass of wine.

After watching the New Orleans Saint Patrick's Day Parade (although there has to be a more exciting word than "watching") and collecting armfuls of ridiculous shit—beer cozies, sunglasses, cabbages, beads—my friend Brett and I followed a slow-moving mass of parade-goers toward someone's house party. It's hard to describe without making it sound horrible—"dozens of tipsy strangers descend upon a home"—but everyone seemed happy and to be having fun. There was a pool out back, and the person there I remember most vividly was a shirtless guy sitting mostly underwater on the pool stairs, wearing swim trunks and a gold-sequined bow tie. He was drinking beer from a green plastic cup, and we talked for a bit. For whatever reason, I asked to take his picture and said that if he told me his email address, I'd remember and eventually send him the photo, which I did. At one point after that, I turned to Brett—he lived there in the city, and I was staying with him—and told him it was the best day of my life. I say that probably more than I should, especially when I've been drinking, but maybe it's always true. Although I don't remember it ever feeling as true as it did then. It felt like if I'd pulled my skin open, sunshine would have poured out. Which sounds ridiculous, but it's the simplest, purest happiness I can recall.

In Maine, on a dock on a lake, thinking about a guy I didn't know if I'd see again. Clouds of baby mosquitoes hovering on the surface of the water. I tried to take their picture before they bit me, but the camera on my phone couldn't focus on them, so the picture was just a blurry gray square. It felt like I was trying to have a very poignant fainting-couch-type moment, all melancholy and alone, but hopeful, or something—a real *woman in the world*. I think I was envisioning something along the lines of when someone you know well positions herself (or himself) in a chair, for instance, with her neck angled back elegantly, or her wrist cocked just so, looking out a window with sunlight streaming in, or whatever it is, pretending she doesn't think anyone's looking, and she looks all beautiful and thoughtful, but you also know that *she* knows she looks all beautiful and thoughtful, just waiting for someone to tell her so, and you want to be like "Oh fuck you, I know what you're doing," but instead you say, "Hey, you look beautiful," and she turns and thanks you, and you momentarily feel like a hero, which then in turn makes you feel like a dick, but anyway. So yeah, I tried to take a picture of the mosquitoes that also incorporated the sunset, so I could post it on Instagram, like, "Look, everyone, I'm in a gorgeous place, but I'm so down-to-earth that I'm focusing on the shitty part." But that never happened and I just went inside and waited for my mom to get out of the shower, or come home from the store or wherever she was. Later on that trip we hiked a very small mountain together, ate plums at the top, and saw a deer in the forest on the way down. She got excited, but I tried to be blasé about it, like, "Oh, I see deer all the time; I'm a big city lady now," or something, but it *was* really neat, and when we passed a group of hikers a couple of minutes later, I worried she might say something to them, like "Keep an eye out for the deer back there," but she didn't. And it's . . . our special deer memory? Ha-ha, no, I have no idea. And actually, she may have said something to the hikers. I don't know why I can't remember. Although I do know for sure that she then started talking about relationships, and I was like, "OMG, Mom, let's talk about the deer again."

I've still never done the thing where you go to an airport late one night with just a passport and a friend, but maybe I will this year. It seems kind of horrible, but maybe that's the point. Or maybe there is no point, to any of this. But maybe THAT's the point. The pointless point. [spins compass]

The Iceland trip was the first time I'd traveled alone and liked it. I didn't even do much—I drank with this person, I met that person from Twitter, I fell asleep, I ate salmon and wandered through supermarkets—but it was so comfortable that I felt like I'd accessed a new kind of freedom. In retrospect, more than at the time, it reminds me of a night when I was twenty-three and out in Manhattan with my friend Bridget and two hot guy-friends of hers, one of whom I had a crush on. We ended up at a twenty-four-hour diner, where Bridget dared me to drink ketchup from the ketchup bottle, I don't remember why. And I remember thinking for a second about how disgusting that would be, to drink ketchup from a bottle, in public, in front of these two hot guys. But also that it would be funny, and that I liked dares. And then something just snapped, or changed, and I realized I didn't care what the hot guys thought of me MORE than what I wanted to do myself, which was to accept the dare and drink the ketchup. So I drank the ketchup, it got all over me, and the hot guys left. But it made me giddy; it felt like a whole new video-game level had just opened up.

ABOUT THE AUTHORS

Chiara Atik (twitter.com/ChiaraAtik) is a New York–based blogger, author, and playwright. Her writing has appeared in *The Hairpin, Gawker,* and *Glamour* magazine as well as on TheAtlantic.com, Today.com (the *Today* show), and Elle.com. She is a writer for MTV's *Hey Girl,* and her play *The Secret Catcher* was produced in 2012. Chiara has been the dating blogger for HowAboutWe since 2010, and her first book, *Modern Dating: A Field Guide,* was published in 2013.

Jim Behrle (twitter.com/behrle) lives in Jersey City, New Jersey. His latest chapbook of poems is called *The Comeback. Ohio Edit* is allegedly collecting everything they can find on the Internet that Behrle has ever done and making a handmade limited edition book called *The Jim Behrle Reader* that will cost, like, $500.

Maria Bustillos (twitter.com/mariabustillos) is a Los Angeles–based writer and critic.

Nicole Cliffe (twitter.com/Nicole_Cliffe) is a writer and the editor of *The Toast*. Her work has been published in *The Hairpin, The Awl, The Morning News,* and *McSweeney's*. She used to work for a quantitative hedge fund but did not have enough access to the money to contribute meaningfully to the 2008 market crash. Canadian by birth, English by some interpretations of constitutional law.

Carrie Frye is a writer and former managing editor of *The Awl*. She blogs at tinglealley .com and tweets @caaf. She currently doesn't have fleas.

Anne Helen Petersen splits her time between teaching media studies at Whitman College in Walla Walla, Washington, and writing things about celebrity and her embarrassing Idaho youth. Her work has been published in *The Hairpin, The Awl, Slate, Lapham's Quarterly,* and *Avidly*. Her first book, *Scandals of Classic Hollywood,* is forthcoming from Plume/ Penguin (spring 2014). She enjoys making vegetables grow in her garden, hanging out in the wilderness, buying old fan magazines off eBay, watching Jeremy Renner movies, and drinking Negronis in her backyard. Find her on Twitter (twitter.com/annehelen) and on her blog, *Celebrity Gossip, Academic Style*, at AnneHelenPetersen.com.

Jenna Wortham (twitter.com/jennydeluxe) is a technology reporter for the *New York Times* who would give anything (literally, anything) to see Blue Ivy IRL. She is also working on a recipe zine and a side project about selfies.

Edith Zimmerman (edithzimmerman.com) is the founding editor of *The Hairpin*.

ACKNOWLEDGMENTS

Thanks to Alex Balk, David Cho, Choire Sicha, and John Shankman.

Kindle Serials

This book was originally released in Episodes as a Kindle Serial. Kindle Serials launched in 2012 as a new way to experience serialized books. Kindle Serials allow readers to enjoy the story as the author creates it, purchasing once and receiving all existing Episodes immediately, followed by future Episodes as they are published. To find out more about Kindle Serials and to see the current selection of Serials titles, visit www.amazon.com/kindleserials.